PREACHING AT THE CROSSROADS

PREACHING AT THE CROSSROADS

HOW THE WORLD—AND OUR PREACHING—IS CHANGING

DAVID J. LOSE

Fortress Press
Minneapolis

PREACHING AT THE CROSSROADS

How the World—and Our Preaching—Is Changing

Cover image: *Cathedral* by Nicholas Wilton

Cover design: Laurie Ingram

Library of Congress Cataloging-in-Publication Data

Print ISBN: 978-0-8006-9973-4

eBook ISBN: 978-1-4514-5229-7

Manufactured in the U.S.A.

This book was produced using PressBooks.com, and PDF rendering was done by PrinceXML.

This book is dedicated with gratitude to Michael Rogness and Karoline Lewis and all the students we've taught together.

CONTENTS

Acknowledgments

The idea of a single author is a convenient myth. Yes, one person often sets pen to paper—or more likely punches on the keys of a laptop—yet there is so much more that goes into bringing the thoughts and ideas of any project to publication. This book is no exception. It was, as I mention in the introduction, in many ways written backwards. Only after I'd written a number of the parts or pieces that eventually furnished the content of this book did I have a chance to look back over the last decade of my work and realize that I had been following—or perhaps, more accurately, bumbling along—a path that had led quite a way from my early training as a preacher. The book now in your hands is the result of taking these various parts and pieces and fashioning them into a coherent whole that I hope not only traces my journey into a very different cultural landscape than the one I had been trained to navigate but also helps other preachers make the same trek. While each chapter was reshaped, rewritten, and in one case written entirely new, I want to mention briefly and thank the persons who listened to or read early versions of these chapters and offered helpful feedback and encouragement along the way.

The first two chapters on postmodernism stem from my dissertation work at Princeton Theological Seminary between 1996 and 2000 under the direction of James Kay, and I remain grateful for his guidance on that project and his continued friendship. I delivered an early, pre-dissertation version of the first chapter at the 1998 annual meeting of the Academy of Homiletics and then a post-dissertation version at the 2005 Festival of Homiletics and soon after at a conference on preaching and worship sponsored by the Diocese of Gothenburg of the Church of Sweden. The second chapter was first delivered at the annual meeting of The Christian Theological Research Fellowship in 1999. At each of those events I enjoyed a number of conversations that helped me think more clearly and practically about the challenges and opportunities of postmodernism.

The third chapter began as a reflection on what it means to confess Christ in a secular world that I offered at the Worship Jubilee conference of the Evangelical Lutheran Church in America in 2007. I turned my attention toward the implications of that work for preaching in response to invitations to preach at Luther Seminary in 2008 and to present at the 2012 Festival of

Homiletics. The fourth chapter has not appeared in any form and stemmed from my work on a grant related to Christian vocation generously funded by the Lilly Endowment. That project, named The Christians Callings in the World, continues to shape, challenge, and energize my work and research.

The fifth and sixth chapters also have their roots in work supported by the Lilly Endowment both in the CCW grant in the Vibrant Congregations Project. Chapter 5 had its origins in conversations about our present-day culture with colleagues at Luther Seminary and was then given form for the first Rethinking Stewardship conference sponsored by Luther Seminary in 2009, an address that was eventually published as a chapter in a *Word and World* Supplemental Issue by the same name.

The heart of the sixth chapter arose from conversations with colleagues and congregation members participating in our grant-related work on congregational vibrancy. An earlier version was also published in *Word and World*, appearing in the 2010 issue on "E-dentity." I am grateful to the journal and its editor, Fred Gaiser, for permission first to present it at the annual meeting of the Academy of Homiletics that same year and now to publish it here.

As I review the history of these chapters, two sets of folks stand out. The first are the good people who have shepherded the Festival of Homiletics into the premiere preaching conference in the country. David Howell, its founder and visionary leader, and Sally Peters, the Director of Lifelong Learning at Luther Seminary who now, with David, oversees and continues to develop it, have been incredibly gracious colleagues, and I am grateful for the opportunities I've had to try out some of my crazier ideas at the Festival.

The second are the stewards of the Lilly Endowment and, in particular, its Religion Division. The research I've been privileged to direct has absolutely transformed my thinking about the call of the church in this day and age and the role preaching may play in responding to that call. Craig Dykstra, John Wimmer, and Chris Coble have each and together supported this work, and I am very grateful to them and their associates.

Since first determining to draw these various pieces into a single narrative, I've been greatly aided by several folks. The excellent team at Fortress Press: Will Bergkamp, Marissa Wold, Olga Lobasenko, Mark Christianson, and Joe Riley in particular have given their time and expertise to seeing this project come to fruition. Jason Misselt of Luther Seminary has provided helpful assistance in tracking down elusive references. And Ronald Allen, of Christian Theological Seminary, and Paul Scott Wilson, of Emmanuel College at the University of Toronto, each read an initial draft of the completed manuscript and provided invaluable feedback that made this book much stronger. I am so grateful for the time they took, the wisdom they shared, and the friendship we've enjoyed over the years.

Finally, a word of thanks to my students and to the two teachers of preaching with whom I have shared my vocation and journey over the last decade, Michael Rogness and Karoline Lewis. They have been constant and supportive conversation partners, great friends, and excellent teachers from whom I've learned a great deal. I gratefully dedicate this book to them and to all the students we have shared teaching.

Introduction: At the Crossroads

When I was twelve, my family and I took a white-water rafting trip down the Roaring Fork River of Colorado. Not content to simply ride along, we opted for the more adventurous route of paddling ourselves. This meant we straddled the pontoon of the raft with one leg inside and one leg dipped into the icy waters of the river. My older sister and I shared the front positions on the raft, and because the first mile or so of the river was fairly gentle, I was lulled into thinking my light straddle of the raft—kind of like the way you would straddle a horse for a trail ride—was adequate. Then we hit a genuine stretch of rapids, and the first wash of the white water swept me into the freezing river.

I started to panic as my breath was ripped away by the ice-cold water. But then I remembered our guide's instructions. I bobbed up out of the river and twisted myself around so that my feet and legs were as close to the surface as possible, a position the raft guides accurately described as "rump bumping."

By the time I had cleared the rapids, I'd been swept a considerable distance out in front of the raft and my family. As the water slowed slightly, I swam to the shore, climbed out, and tried to walk alongside the river, hoping to catch sight of the group. But the shore soon became a steep embankment as the river churned ahead into a gulley and the water's speed picked up once more. So I climbed up the embankment and found myself in the middle of a large swath of rolling green pasture. "Excellent," I thought. "I can walk above the white water until we're out of the ravine, and I'll have a great view of the river the whole time." It was the first bit of luck since I'd been swept overboard.

My enthusiasm quickly ebbed after a few hundred yards, though, as I crested one of those beautiful rolling hills and came across a bull. Actually, it was not just a bull, but a huge black bull like nothing I'd ever seen outside of a movie. And it was standing right in the middle of my path. Though that day was a good thirty-five years ago, I remember keenly the realization that I'd come to a crossroads. I could either try to sneak past the bull as it contentedly chewed on the grass or else backtrack, slide down the embankment, and reenter the cold white water. Knowing next to nothing about what makes a bull take interest in someone, I chose the latter and hurried back into the river.

THE ~~PROBLEM~~ MYSTERY OF PREACHING

Sometimes when we reach a crossroads, it's obvious. Maybe it's because we're at an actual crossing of two paths, each marked clearly. Or maybe the either-or quality of the situation is obvious, as it was when I encountered the bull. In both cases, we know where we are, and the decision we have to make is clear.

Sometimes, however, we realize we reached a crossroads only well after we've made the decision and chosen a route—accepting this particular congregational call, for instance, or ending a relationship, or starting a family. Even when the decision in front of us is significant, we may not realize how completely it will alter our future.

And sometimes we suspect we're at a crossroads but can't tell for sure. We may feel the pressure that comes with making a momentous decision, yet be unable to identify exactly what juncture we've come to or the options we are called to decide between. We sense there's no going back but can't quite trace the path that brought us here, so we have a hard time deciphering what "back" and "forward" even mean.

More and more preachers I talk to fall into this last category. They feel that all kinds of things are changing, but they can't quite put their finger on precisely what. They feel they are less effective than they once were, but they aren't sure why. They know they received good training at seminary, and often have being going back for continuing education regularly, yet have lost confidence that they know what they're doing. And most pernicious of all, even when they preach a "really good sermon" (you know, the kind that gets way more than average "Good sermon, Pastor" comments), they're not sure it's what the congregation really needs anymore.

Sometimes, even when a sense of the decision in front of us becomes fairly concrete (use PowerPoint, for instance, or abandon the lectionary in favor of sermon series), we may feel as if the choices themselves are only symptoms of something much larger. As one pastor I spoke with put it, the options she is regularly offered for enlivening her preaching too often feel like gimmicks, rearranging deck chairs on the *Titanic* while the ship continues to take on water.

I've been preaching now for nearly twenty-five years and teaching preaching for a little more than half that time, and the refrain I've heard from preachers from across Christian traditions and from every generation is the same: *preaching is broken*. This is usually followed by an earnest plea: *fix it!*

And for more than a decade, I've tried to do so in the classroom and the pulpit, at conferences, lectures, and workshops. Of late, however, the conclusion I've reached is that preaching *can't* be fixed. Not because I've given up on preaching, mind you, but rather because I've become deeply suspicious of the analysis and the corresponding request. Let me try to explain.

My suspicion has two sources. The first is my familiarity with the literature on preaching. Since at least the 1960s, you see, homileticians have been responding to the charge that preaching is broken by coming up with a variety of fixes. The catalogue of diagnosed problems and prescribed solutions is almost endless:

- *Problem:* Preaching is too much like a dull university lecture to engage audiences that have grown up in the entertainment age. *Solution:* Move from didactic and deductive styles to narrative, inductive forms of preaching.
- *Problem:* Preaching isn't trusted as a form of communication in an era that is suspicious of authority. *Solution:* Move out of the pulpit, involve people in your preparation, and take up an egalitarian style and tone.
- *Problem:* Preaching offers too much information in an age already swimming in data. *Solution:* Abandon information, and instead strive to cultivate an experience through the preaching event.
- *Problem:* Preachers can't compete with the likes of David Letterman or Jimmy Fallon. *Solution:* Abandon the manuscript, and adopt a more conversational style of preaching.
- *Problem:* Preaching itself seems dated in an age where the image is everything. *Solution:* Put up a screen and incorporate slides and movie clips into your sermon.

And the list goes on.

At this point, I should be clear: It's not that there haven't been a number of helpful analyses of the challenges preachers face or a host of creative responses. I've incorporated many of these suggestions into my own preaching. Yet the problems with preaching persist.

Perhaps, I've begun to wonder, that's because of the very nature of preaching. If we are called to proclaim good news that is not just old news or the daily news but regularly surprises and even arrests our hearers, then perhaps preachers should not be surprised by the inherent and unending challenge of doing that. As theologian Joseph Sittler asserted a half century ago, "Of course preaching is in trouble. Whence did we ever manufacture the assumption that it was ever to be in anything but trouble" if it is to be relevant to a changing world and faithful to the troubling gospel of Jesus Christ?[1] Preaching, that is, if it is faithful to the gospel, will always be somewhat broken as it seeks to give fit testimony to the one broken upon the cross.

I have a hunch, though, that there's also something more going on. If my only suspicion of requests to fix preaching were that preaching will always be somewhat broken, I would be content with the ongoing stream of homiletical resources currently available. Indeed, I would be eager to add to them, hoping to address the particular concern I've identified and provide a helpful angle of vision and recommendation.

But I don't think that's what's needed at this point, which brings me to my second area of concern about the decades-old pattern of identifying and analyzing the broken element of preaching and proposing a fix. This problem-solution analysis, I've come to believe, underestimates the scope and depth of the changes we've been experiencing and therefore fundamentally refuses to call into question the essential practice of preaching itself. As long as we're trying to "fix" preaching, that is, we've already concluded that the basic practice and patterns of preaching we've employed in recent decades—and, truth be told, for centuries—are essentially sound. They don't need to be redefined, only revised. And I'm just not sure that's the case anymore.

Let me try to get at this from another angle by borrowing the helpful distinction sometimes made between a problem and a mystery. A *problem*, according to this point of view, is a challenge or need that has a recognized context, involves set limits and variables, and presents itself for solution. Typically, the key task in solving problems is amassing more information and, based on careful analysis of that information, making changes at the level of technique or practice. We are, I believe, by evolutionary disposition and professional training born problem solvers. This is regularly an immensely helpful trait, as there are all kinds of important problems in desperate need of solution. But because we are best equipped to solve problems, we often reduce *everything* to a problem to be solved, and then we proceed in appropriate fashion.[2]

Sometimes, however, the context is no longer recognizable, so we don't know the limits and variables involved. In short, sometimes the rules of the very game we are playing change, and in this situation, more information not only doesn't help us but may actually confuse us by inducing us to operate by the

1. Joseph Sittler, *The Anguish of Preaching* (Philadelphia: Fortress Press, 1966; Chicago: Evangelical Lutheran Church in America, 2008), 14.

2. See, for instance, Malcom Gladwell's essay, "Enron, Intelligence, and the the Perilds of Too Much Information," in *What the Dog Saw and Other Adventures* (New York: Little, Brown, and Company, 2009), esp. 153–55.

rules of the old context rather than take seriously the foreign terrain in which we find ourselves. These types of challenges are better termed *mysteries*. And as much as we theological types love the *idea* of mystery, we—like just about everyone else—find the actual condition of living in mystery to be challenging.

Why? Because mysteries, other than the whodunit type, can't be solved. Rather, mysteries can only be embraced. They don't require more information, but rather a curious mind and a willingness to suspend past assumptions and judgments in order to be surprised by what manifests itself in this new context and world. That is what makes mysteries so vexing: to the degree that we are wed to past practices that succeeded in a different context, a mystery makes us feel either frustrated or incompetent—and all too often a bit of both.

That's why I'm suspicious of the pattern of homiletical research that treats preaching as a problem to be fixed. I increasingly think what confronts us is not a problem but a mystery. The context in which we live, move, and have our being in ministry has changed so significantly that I suspect we don't really know what will work to promote a lively engagement with the Christian faith today. That doesn't rule out having our hunches and trying out some new practices. But these efforts are, we should admit, experiments, for we don't yet know what kind of preaching will best serve us in equipping Christians to live in a post-Christian world. Why? Because Christians haven't operated in a world like this for more than fifteen hundred years!

For this reason, I firmly believe that our call at this juncture is not to solve the problems of our church but instead to embrace the mystery of the world in which we find ourselves, trusting that if we do so with open and courageous hearts, appropriate ways of being and acting—including the act of preaching—will present themselves. So if the task of fashioning a homiletic appropriate to our age eludes us at present, perhaps that's because we haven't yet sufficiently embraced the mysterious new world in which we live and to which we are called to preach. Our dreams of continuing on the high road and navigating familiar if also challenging green pastures is no longer available to us. Instead, we need to slide down the muddy banks of this curious world and clamber back into the cold water to see where the brisk cultural currents will take us.

Actually, that's not quite right. It's not that treading the familiar path is unavailable, but rather that it also entails significant risk. Perhaps the risk isn't as great as getting gored by a big black bull, but then again, perhaps in other ways, it may be even greater. For if we continue to embrace patterns of preaching designed and suited for a bygone age, then we probably shouldn't be surprised if the new age in which we live continues to pass us by. The choice is before us.

We are at a crossroads—one where not only the outcome is unclear, but also the primary challenge and perhaps even the alternatives. We can either continue adapting and refining established techniques or be willing to call into question our fundamental practices by leaning into and listening carefully to the world in front of us.

QUESTIONS OF THE AGE

This book is an attempt to choose the route of leaning in and listening. It does so by giving attention to three dominant ways of describing the changes that have shaped and continue to influence our culture and world over the last half century: postmodernism, secularism, and pluralism. My guess is that we all have at least a passing familiarity with these terms and wouldn't dispute that they are central elements of our current culture and world. But getting a handle on the challenges they present is another matter altogether. It's one thing to say we live in a postmodern world, but it's another to allow that knowledge to shape our preaching so as to respond to that world.

To help us embrace and respond to these three dimensions of our time, I want to hearken back to an observation made by Paul Tillich. Tillich once divided world history into three distinct phases based on the dominant question of the age. For the ancient world, Tillich argued, the question was one of life and death: How does one escape the finality of death to enjoy life eternal? In the Middle Ages, the question changed to one of guilt and forgiveness: Given original sin, how do we find a merciful God who will overlook our guilt and offer us forgiveness? In the modern era, in which and for which Tillich wrote, the conversation had moved to existential questions of meaninglessness and meaning: How do I make sense of my life and find my place in the world?[3]

What I like about Tillich's approach is that it invites us to look at the evolving history of the Christian tradition not as a series of solutions to different problems but rather as an ongoing, curious, and lively engagement with the questions that people living at particular times were asking. Tillich, in other words, was suggesting that Christian theology, at its best, embraces the mystery of the culture in which it finds itself so it can understand, appreciate, and ultimately speak into that mystery in ways that are appropriate and helpful.

For this reason, I will try in this introduction to introduce briefly each of these three cultural elements or movements that have defined our time—postmodernism, secularism, and pluralism—in terms of the central questions they are raising. This will help us not only to understand each

---

3. See Tillich's *The Courage To Be*, 2nd ed. (New Haven: Yale University Press, 2000), esp. pp. 40–53.

movement better on its own terms but also to differentiate the movements from each other, as they overlap and shape each other at many points. Thinking about these different movements in terms of questions will also help us identify some of the primary challenges and opportunities that each movement presents to us as preachers.

When it comes to *postmodernism*, the primary question is *epistemological*: How do we know for certain whether anything is true? Hence, the primary challenge that postmodernism presents is whether we can speak honestly and intelligibly about truth in a world of competing truth claims. As we'll see, postmodernists are fairly skeptical about our ability to do so. Indeed, it is precisely this skepticism about discovering, let alone describing, objective truth—the goal that coalesced in the Enlightenment and was prosecuted across modernity—that marks the period as postmodern. The casualty of such skepticism has been certainty, the belief that we can know anything for sure. But the possibility latent in such loss is the rediscovery of a vibrant faith that rests not on objective data but on the confessions, truth claims, and shared experiences of the Christian community.

Contrary to postmodernism, *secularism* has not rebelled against the notion of truth but rather against the idea that truth is rooted in God. Secularism accepts the modern impulse to consign religion to the private sphere of our lives and takes that to its natural conclusion—determining that religion, and therefore the God that animates it, has little to no place in the public sphere. Hence, secularism is marked first and foremost by a *loss of transcendence* and the conviction that what we see around us, the material and physical world, is finally all there us. This materialism, while it flourished for a few decades, has more recently induced a crisis of hope, a growing conviction that whatever our advances, we cannot validate our material pursuits as legitimate, let alone worthwhile. The questions of the secular age are therefore more existential: Where do we find hope? Do my life and my labor have any enduring value or meaning?

The challenge Christian preachers have faced since the Enlightenment and increasingly with the full blooming of the secular age in the late twentieth century has been to justify the transcendent claims of Christianity in light of the more immanent standards of human reason. But as the secular story has fallen short, providing a too-limited view of human life, preachers have the opportunity to offer hearers hope rooted in the audacious claims of the biblical story, in this way not only recovering a palpable sense of hope but also reclaiming much of our ordinary lives as arenas in which we can experience the ongoing work of God to love and bless the world.

Pluralism, the third element of our cultural landscape I want to explore, emerged as the great paradox of a secular age that ended up being, against most predictions, highly religious age. But that religiousness is of a distinctly different character than the one our parents knew. Faced with a plethora of religious and spiritual options, as well as a host of other meaning-making narratives, Christians who could not adopt a conservative isolationism in relation to the pluralistic culture in which we live have developed a more cosmopolitan outlook that stresses the value of all religious views. Whatever the intrinsic value of such an open-minded position, the downside has been an increasing inability to name the distinctiveness of Christianity. This has resulted in a corresponding loss of Christian identity that has had grave consequences for church attendance. As people find themselves nearly overwhelmed by the number of opportunities and obligations presented to them, and absent a sense of the distinctiveness or utility of the Christian narrative, they have increasingly chosen to do something other than worship at church on Sunday morning, something presumably more meaningful to them than listening to well-crafted sermons and singing classic hymns.

The pressing questions of the pluralistic age therefore take shape around identity, both individual and communal: What does it mean to be Christian? How does the Christian story help me make sense of and navigate my life? In a world saturated by meaning-making stories, how do we pass ours on? Despite the numerous challenges that arise from living in a world of many faiths and stories, there are also significant opportunities for preachers. In particular, if we take seriously the possibility that preaching is not only called to proclaim the hope-creating promises of the gospel but also to help believers own and articulate those promises for themselves, we may not only reconfigure preaching but also fashion a useful and compelling Christian identity for this and future generations.

The Path Forward

We are, I believe, at a crossroads. My hope through this book is to help us identify this crossroads more clearly so that we can make a faithful decision about which path to take forward.

To get us started down this path, my intention is to address each of these three cultural movements in two chapters. In chapters 1, 3, and 5, I will first sketch the contours of postmodernism, secularism, and pluralism, respectively, in order to offer an initial theological and homiletical response. In chapters 2, 4, and 6, I will isolate a distinct and concrete dimension of each respective movement in order to offer preachers more focused suggestions on how to preach in this day and age. In this way, I hope to offer a straightforward analysis of the age in which we live and concrete suggestions for preaching into it so we may embrace the mystery of our age and respond with sermons that are as fitting to our culture as they are faithful to the gospel.

But while that's the simple and straightforward story, it's not the most accurate one. Truth be told, this book was written backward. Most books, you see, start when the author has an idea, thesis, or argument, which the author then articulates in the writing process. But in this case, I realized on the plane home from a conference just over a year ago that my own sense of preaching had changed significantly over the last decade. This wasn't a complete surprise; I knew I was teaching differently and that the focus of my writing had shifted. But on that plane ride, I realized just how far I'd wandered from what I'd originally been taught.

When I got home, I started looking at some of the work of the last decade and discovered that the significant twists and turns of my journey as a preacher could be traced through a few key pieces I'd written. One or two of these were published in theological journals, but the others were conference addresses, classroom lecturers, and sermons. As I read through them, I realized I'd been attending to these issues of postmodernism, secularism, and pluralism for some time, long before I'd actually found names for them.

Once I'd named my own journey in this way, my hope was to pull together and organize these various pieces and get them quickly off to a publisher. But it wasn't that easy. While I'd written them as stand-alone pieces, when I placed them side by side they began talking to each other so that I had to go back and revise (and in some cases, completely rewrite) earlier work to allow this conversation greater coherence and unity.

What you have before you is the final result—not "final" in the sense that I've figured it all out, but rather in the sense that I am finally satisfied that these six chapters, now presented as a sustained narrative rather than a collection of essays, sketch the world in which we live and preach, a world that is strikingly different than the one for which I was trained. But while I am sometimes daunted by the challenges of this strange new world, I have also come to take great delight in it, reveling in its mystery and energized by the opportunities it presents. I hope that after reading these pages, you too will come to know better, respect, and delight in the mystery of this age, knowing that this is precisely the world that God loves so very much.

PART I

Postmodernism

1

Preaching at the End of the World (as We Know It)

Whether you are reading various preaching and theological periodicals, church growth literature, journalistic magazines like the *Atlantic,* or almost anything else that comments on our contemporary culture, you've probably been struck by the degree to which all of them agree on at least one thing: our world is changing, and changing faster than at any period in recent history.

Depending on their audience, various authors and commentators may refer to these cultural shifts in different ways. Those in the church will speak of a post-Christian or post-Constantinian age. Others in business will refer to the post-industrialized world or the silicon age. Still others will indicate the distinctive character of emerging generations with labels such as GenX or the Millennial Generation. Whatever the terms employed, the shared conviction is that we live in an age of enormous societal and cultural change. And of all the various labels and handles people have tried out to capture these changes, probably the most frequent descriptor used in recent years is *postmodern.* While the term is now fairly commonplace, many church leaders and preachers—not to mention the cultural pundits themselves!—continue to grapple with what it actually means and what it implies for preaching.

For this reason, we begin our exploration of preaching at the crossroads at the intersection of modernist certainty and postmodern skepticism. Despite the suspicions, if not outright hostility, many Christian leaders harbor toward postmodernity, I believe it offers more opportunities than challenges. Indeed, I am convinced it offers preachers the best chance for offering a lively witness to, and gaining an engaged hearing of, the gospel that we've had in several centuries.

I offer the reasons for my confidence in the next three sections of this chapter. In the first, I will sketch the broad contours of the movement—what makes postmodernity actually *post*modern. In the second, I will address the central challenge the movement poses Christian preachers: the nature of our access to truth. In the third, I will describe several elements of preaching affected by postmodern theory that may help us offer our witness to the gospel faithfully and effectively in this day and age. Finally, in a fourth section, I will conclude with a few thoughts—and, truth be told, exhortations—on the need for postmodern courage.

PUTTING THE "POSTMODERN AGE" IN PERSPECTIVE

Of the three elements of the cultural zeitgeist I have named, postmodernism is perhaps the broadest, most currently pervasive, and probably least understood of the movements we've set ourselves to face. For this reason, it often feels both omnipresent and indecipherable. Curiously, the chief difficulty in coming to grips with the nature and implications of postmodernity is its very name, which is as ungainly and confusing as any descriptive tag we've heard in recent years.

In particular, it's difficult for many of us to sort out what "postmodern" can mean when we regularly associate the word *modern* with whatever is most contemporary, current, or up-to-date. That is, how can something that exists now be "post-today"? But when cultural theorists, philosophers, and others employ the term *modern*, they refer not to whatever is most current but rather to a distinct historical era of the Western world.[1] For this reason, it will be helpful to consider briefly some of the characteristics of the modern age in order to appreciate what *post*modernity is seeking to move beyond.[2]

MODERNITY IN A NUTSHELL

Inaugurated in the middle of the seventeenth century in the aftermath of the Thirty Years' War, the modern era represented a shift from grounding one's basic assumptions about the world and society largely on religious faith to doing so based solely on human reason. This shift had significant implications, as it dramatically affected the criteria the leading intellectuals of the day—and later the larger populace—used to determine what is true, reliable, and valid.

In the ancient world, the standards for legitimacy (that is, the means by which one validates what is undeniably true) were twofold: coherency

---

1. It is important to note that both modernity and postmodernity are Western constructs. That is, they describe the intellectual history largely of Europe and North America and cannot easily be applied to other regions and cultures of the world.

2. This discussion of postmodernity and its relation to modernity draws from the first chapter of my dissertation work published as *Confessing Jesus Christ: Preaching in a Postmodern World* (Grand Rapids: Eerdmans, 1993).

and fidelity. Coherency means your theory had to make sense and not have any logical contradictions; fidelity means it could not contradict previously validated traditions. For instance, when the Protestant Reformers made their case before the pope, emperor, and general populace, they consistently offered arguments that were logically sound and based on interpretations of Scripture and church tradition, suggesting that, far from doing anything new, their understanding of these ancient authorities was actually more accurate and more faithful than that of their opponents. Practitioners from across disciplines employed similar criteria.

After the devastating religious wars of the seventeenth century, however, intellectual and cultural leaders despaired of understanding and ordering the world and human society via a shared but disputed religious tradition. We should be clear, at this point, that by reaching this conclusion, the early modernists were *not* rejecting faith; most continued to be faithful members of the church. Rather, they were rejecting the use of religious dogma as an adequate foundation on which to base their theories about the nature of the world. The difficulty they immediately faced, however, is that one needs some kind of self-evident and indisputable foundation in order to develop indisputable criteria by which to arbitrate between competing truth claims in order to construct any reliable theories about the nature of the world.[3] For this reason, simply rejecting religious or dogmatic foundations was not enough; they had to seek out another, more reliable footing upon which to erect theories about the natural and social world. In this pursuit, they turned from faith to reason, shifting their attention from speculation about the Creator to earnest study of the creation.[4]

As a result, there soon emerged a single standard of legitimacy: rational verifiability. That is, the architects of modernity demanded that all conclusions about the observable world be reached through the careful application of human reason such that any other rational person employing similar means would reach the same conclusion. The promised reward of this methodology was knowledge about the world that was entirely objective and universally valid. The modernists pursued this goal with a passion, believing that the discovery and use of such knowledge would benefit all humanity.[5] This pursuit of

---

3. See Stephen Toulmin, *Cosmopolis: The Hidden Agenda of Modernity* (Chicago: University of Chicago Press, 1990), esp. 45–87.

4. In fact, it was the precisely their faith in an intelligent and benevolent Creator that greatly spurred the early modernists' attempts to understand and harness a creation that reflected both the goodness and rationality of its Creator. On this, see Diogenes Allen, *Christian Belief in a Postmodern World: The Full Wealth of Conviction* (Louisville: Westminster/John Knox, 1989), 23–34.

knowledge, in turn, gave birth to the scientific method and the rise of the industrial, mechanical, medical, and technological revolutions that followed, all of which are based on the premise that one can trust only those conclusions that can be studied, replicated, and thereby verified by agreed-upon standards of human rationality.

After a brief though distinct period of anxiety (after all, it's not easy to abandon one's basic view of how to make sense of the world), the modern era came to be dominated by a pervasive optimism that through the diligent application of reason, humans could solve most of the world's problems. And indeed—as witnessed by the development of modern medicine, which has limited the impact of many previously deadly diseases, and the advent of modern farming, which has greatly increased food production, to cite just two examples—the confidence, energy, and ingenuity of modern thinkers has produced dramatic benefits.

By the late twentieth century, however, more and more persons came to believe that, whatever its benefits, the modern view of the world has also exacted tremendous costs. To name only a few of the "disappointments" of the modern age, poverty has not been eradicated, wars have not ceased, in the place of old diseases we have new and deadlier ones (and some of the old ones are reappearing more virulent than ever), and after three centuries of harvesting the world's resources to meet the demands of technological advancement, our world stands on the brink of environmental disaster. In light of all this, modernist confidence has waned, if not been extinguished, and there has arisen in its place a distinct skepticism about claims of the sufficiency of human reason to solve all problems and meet every need.

THE POSTMODERN REACTION

It is this skepticism, in fact, that marks the current age as *post*modern. Postmodernists seek to move beyond what they believe was the naive, self-serving, and ultimately destructive optimism of modernity. In particular, postmodernists dispute the claim that there are neutral, self-evident, and universal foundations one can appeal to for determining what is true. Rather, they contend that all our theories—as well as the way in which such theories are implemented in the sphere of human relations—are influenced by preconceptions we hold based on our race, gender, nationality, religion, economic status, previous experience, and other factors that even the most exacting methods cannot entirely rule out.

5. Ibid., 5.

In short, according to postmodern critics, there is no rational foundation that guarantees absolute objectivity or neutrality. To put it another way, there is no "God's-eye view" that allows us to view all sides of any particular issue with absolute impartiality. Ultimately, they contend, there is no way to get around the phenomenon that we see what we see and believe what we believe in part because of where we are standing at the time. Hence, postmodernists are aptly described as "antifoundational," rejecting any neutral, objective, and ultimate court of appeal by which to adjudicate between competing truth claims.

In contrast to the modernist quest for self-evident foundations and timeless truth, therefore, postmodernists argue that whatever theories, or even constructions, about reality that are rife with our own unacknowledged biases and turn out to be, ultimately, made up as much by convictions and beliefs as they are by evidence. The chief impulse and duty of the postmodern critic, then, is not merely to point out the unquestioned beliefs that lie quietly beneath our various worldviews, but also to draw such unacknowledged convictions out into the open for public scrutiny and evaluation.

Further, postmodernists are eager to point out the degree of hostility and even violence directed at those who dare question such constructions of reality and thereby challenge the status quo. The history of the Western world, they argue, is one long, distressing story of the consistent quelling, if not outright quashing, of dissident voices that refuse to conform to the order established by those in power. From Galileo and Copernicus to Susan B. Anthony and Martin Luther King Jr., those who call into question the culture's basic sense of what is undeniably true—whether in the world of science, politics, religion, or social relations—inevitably risk their reputations and even their very lives. A secondary impulse of postmodernists is therefore to resist the modernist desire for uniformity and conformity that has all too often been achieved through the use of force.

What we soon come to realize, then, is that the term *postmodern* does not designate a particular discipline or isolated movement so much as it describes a more general attitude of unrelenting skepticism pervading a number of disciplines concerning the validity of previously held assumptions about the nature, and even existence, of objective truth.

POSTMODERN CONVICTIONS

The extent of the gap between modernist certainty and postmodern skepticism becomes clear when we examine the distinct shifts in perspective regarding the nature of reality, truth, language, and power. Indeed, examining these contested elements outlines what we might regard as widely held postmodern convictions.

First, whereas modernists seek to describe reality, postmodernists deny the existence of a singular reality, speaking instead of the various competing "metanarratives" or "standard stories," one of which we unconsciously adopt and unquestioningly take as our reality. Only when confronted with an alternative do we become aware of the parameters of our own cultural-linguistic worldview, and then usually only long enough to dispute and oppose the alternative vision.

Second, while modernists searched for ultimate truth, postmodernists argue that what we call "truth" is simply the name we attach to those values the dominant culture has tacitly agreed upon. Truth, according to the postmodernist, is a social construct. After all, what any given culture has posited as undeniably, even self-evidently true has changed from generation to generation; what remains constant is the need to affirm one's present values as the one and only Truth.

Third, while modernists view language as entirely descriptive, a neutral tool by which to describe Reality, postmodernists see language (and culture) as inherently productive, the raw material from which we fashion our worldview. This is why the names we use to describe those who are different from us are so important. The language we employ—positive or negative, affirming or pejorative—simultaneously creates and limits our capacity to experience those persons.

Finally, while modernists believe that one attains power by aligning oneself with reality (hence Francis Bacon's "knowledge is power"), postmodernists assert that it is actually those who wield power in the culture who get to name what counts for knowledge and therefore to determine what is legitimate, true, and real. For this reason, Michel Foucault reversed Bacon's dictum and declared instead that "power is knowledge."[6]

While this clash of ideas and worldviews has raged for several decades in academic institutions, by the turn of the millennium it had seeped deeply into the popular culture. Films like *Pulp Fiction*, *The Matrix*, and *Fight Club*

---

6. Foucault's conception of the relationship between power and knowledge is complex and evolved throughout his career, but the following statement is fairly representative of his unique contribution: "We should admit that power produces knowledge (and not simply by encouraging it because it serves power, or by applying it because it is useful); that power and knowledge directly imply one another; that there is no power relation without the correlative constitution of a field of knowledge, nor any knowledge that does not presuppose and constitute at the same time power relations." *Discipline and Punish: The Birth of the Prison*, trans. Alan Sheridan (London: Penguin, 1977), 27.

near the turn of the millennium, and *Inception, The Tree of Life,* and *Life of Pi* more recently, all portray postmodern skepticism and values not simply as the norm but as desirable for navigating a world where you cannot trust what is presented as real. Similarly, television shows like *Lost, Mad Men,* and numerous "reality" television programs play with our sense of reality, trace the antecedents of our preference for image over substance, and even invite the question of whether there is anything more than image in the first place. Throughout, these and other art forms acknowledge the deep distrust of received values and traditions that was percolating in our culture during the second half of the twentieth century and now has boiled over, calling into question any singular, comprehensive view of truth and reality.

In light of all these philosophical and cultural shifts, it is little wonder that so many find themselves confused, worried, and even threatened. In the postmodern world, it can feel as if just about everything we once cherished as true is now up for grabs, if not actually under assault. Indeed, the relentless onslaught of postmodern skepticism quickly provokes the question "Is *anything* true?" The answer we give to that question will have significant implications for our preaching in a postmodern age.

Telling the Truth in a Postmodern World

Although the challenges postmodernism offers Christian preachers and theologians are many, most can by grouped together under the overarching charge that postmodernism denies there is any universal Truth available to us. If truth, like beauty, is entirely in the eye of the beholder, and if we would therefore be better to abandon the word altogether in favor of less ambitious ones like *value* or *meaning*, then those of us charged with proclaiming the gospel—a message we believe is true in all times and places—find ourselves rendered nearly mute.

Or do we? A more careful read of the postmodern critique of modernity reveals that postmodernists are not so much against truth in and of itself as they are against claims and assertions of *self-evident* truth. Once you declare something self-evident, you immediately place it beyond the pale of critical review and privilege it above all other assertions. Such a move is inherently a power play, as it gives one voice all the power in the conversation and greatly restricts the freedom of anyone else to even question the assertion.

Postmodernists not only resist this move, however; they also ask whether it is necessary in the first place. Modernity, they contend, was built upon the false premise that in order to make sense of the world, you need an absolute bedrock foundation upon which to build your theories. Only if you begin with something immune to the tumults of changing religious beliefs or shifting philosophical convictions, modernists believed, can you build anything that will last.

Postmodernists respond by suggesting that perhaps our foundations do not need to be quite so rigid or permanent in order for us to build with confidence. As evidence, they point to the number of times modernist foundations have changed. Whether it was notions of the superiority of one race, gender, or religious tradition over another or a particular theory about the structure of the physical world, when the reigning foundational assumption was challenged or proved to be inadequate, it was merely revised or replaced, and the world did not end.[7] Rather, we modernists simply revised our views, incorporated the new data, and kept on building our comprehensive theories about the nature of reality. While some revisions—particularly those regarding our notions of social equality—were more tumultuous than others, none has yet proved fatal.

Certainly, we in the church—who have over the centuries weathered controversies over issues as far-ranging as slavery, the ordination of women, the proper observance of the Sabbath, the appropriate Christian response to war, and human sexuality, just to name a few—can appreciate that it is possible to change, adapt, and even reverse one's previous beliefs and still remain intact.[8] The change is sometimes difficult, occurs over great lengths of time, and creates rifts among believers. Nevertheless, the church has consistently weathered and even flourished amid significant change. Ironically, though we acknowledge that many of the controversies of previous ages seem now at the very least to be settled and at times even to be a bit embarrassing, we have difficulty viewing our present struggles with similar good humor or the confidence that we will survive this tumult as well. Why?

Postmodernists would suggest it is because ultimate foundations bolster our sense that the world is an ordered, stable, sensible environment and thereby provide social stability, something we often unconsciously prize even above fidelity. The difficulty with posing ultimate foundations, however, is that we can become so invested in defending these for the sake of preserving stability and order that we not only ignore the fact that we cannot prevent social, cultural, and intellectual tumults but also lose sight of the edifice we are constructing in the first place. Postmodern thought suggests that, rather than

---

7. See Jacques Derrida, "Structure, Sign, and Play in the Discourse of the Human Sciences," in *Writing and Difference*, trans. Alan Bass (Chicago: University of Chicago Press, 1978), esp. 278–79.

8. For an excellent set of case studies of such controversies, see Willard M. Swartley, *Slavery, Sabbath, War, and Women: Case Issues in Biblical Interpretation* (Scottdale, PA: Herald, 1983).

build permanent and rigid foundations, we instead learn from architects in the San Francisco Bay area who have discovered that buildings with more flexible foundations are more likely to survive seismic tremors.

The postmodern proposal therefore is not that we abandon philosophical foundations altogether, but that we offer them as penultimate, rather than ultimate, conclusions. In other words, though we believe our foundations to be true, we are open to the possibility that they may need to be revised in light of new data, experience, or more plausible alternatives. Adopting more flexible, penultimate foundations grants the possibility of future adaptation while preserving enough stable ground upon which to build useful theories about the nature of our world.

As an example, we might point to that quintessential of modern disciplines, mathematics, noting that at the heart of every mathematical proof are axioms, unproven—indeed, unprovable—assertions. Yet mathematicians are not paralyzed until their axioms are proven eternally valid; rather, they act *as if* they are true and build their various theorems, pausing to reconsider their work only at those points where their axiomatic assumptions are called into question by emerging data. When challenged by another theorist, a mathematician would, of course, defend his or her conclusions and demand good logic and an abundance of evidence. But no mathematician would deny the right of another to call into question either the theorem or the axiom upon which it stands. To do so would lose the benefit of constructive critique that might ultimately improve the theory in question. In a similar way, postmodernists invite us to take the same approach to our various philosophical and theological foundations, refusing to place them beyond critical review, revision, and even reversal, hoping in this way not only to end the spiral of violence modernity sponsored but also to increase the utility—dare we say truthfulness?—of the theories we offer.

This discussion sheds considerable light on our questions about truth. For if there is some merit to the postmodern argument, then we are not forced to *abandon* truth but only to reconsider how we understand it. In particular, we need to perceive that, ultimately, truth is a matter less of final proof than of faithful confession.[9] Our task as Christian theologians and preachers is not to *prove* the faith claims we make (ever the modernist penchant) but instead to witness to the truth we perceive. Of course, we marshal the most compelling evidence and make clear the good reasons for our belief, yet we never assume we have proved it once and for all.

9. I take up the subject of "confession" in far greater depth in *Confessing Jesus Christ*.

This shift from proof to confession, witness, and testimony aligns closely with the biblical witness and much of the church's history. As Christians, we are called, after all, to live as we have been saved, by "faith alone" (Rom. 3:23-28; Eph. 2:8-9), and faith, according to the biblical witness, "is the assurance of things hoped for, the conviction of things not seen" (Heb. 11:1). Further, opting for faithful confession over rational proof opens up new vistas for meaningful dialogue with those who do not share our religious convictions. For when one adopts unrelentingly the language of proof, then anyone who disagrees is immediately an opponent, as proof sees any challenge as a threat. For example, if I am bent on proving that Abraham Lincoln is the greatest U.S. president and you disagree, then my proof is not complete until you either change your mind or I discount your opinion as somehow faulty or unworthy. The legitimacy of proof, to put it another way, rests in its reception, and as long as anyone disagrees with what we are trying to prove, the truth of our assertion is at risk.

Confession, however, operates differently. Its validity rests with the integrity of the confession itself. Consider the following example. When you confess that you love someone (particularly for the first time), you are naturally quite invested in the response of your beloved. Yet whether that response is positive or negative, the integrity of your confession is never in doubt. The integrity—indeed, the validity and legitimacy—of confession rests not with the receiver but with the confessor. Further, even if your beloved has rejected your love, he or she does not suddenly become your opponent. In fact, if that were the case, most of us would be highly suspicious of the quality and caliber of the love professed in the first place. And to return to the earlier illustration, if I shift my desire from proving Lincoln's greatness to confessing it and even defending it, then disagreement is no longer threatening. Now the validity of my assertion rests on the integrity with which I've made it, not on its being universally accepted. In fact, disagreement might even be productive, helping me understand the subject at hand more deeply through our conversation and thereby enabling me to offer a more compelling confession at some later point.

Something analogous is happening when it comes to religious truth. We can confess the truths we believe, give good reasons for them, and yet allow others to disagree, trusting that the most important thing about our claims is not their acceptance by everyone else but rather the integrity of our confession. At this point, however, let me be clear: this does not mean we do not really believe what we say we believe. Rather, it means we will not coerce agreement or belief from others in order to preserve our confidence that what we believe has been proven once and for all and therefore is worthy of our faith. Our job is to testify; it is up to God to make that testimony potent.

In this refusal to take the "power road" of rational proof, we echo the work of God in Jesus Christ on the cross, taking the path of weakness and trusting in ultimate vindication (see Phil. 2:6-11). Further, we perceive an inescapably eschatological element to our notions of truth, as we recognize that Jesus and the ultimate truth he represents and embodies always stand just beyond our reach, moving toward us and beckoning us forward but refusing to be held captive by any particular age, tradition, or believer (see 1 Cor. 13:12). Truth, as it turns out, can be *confessed* and *professed* but never *possessed*. And while this kind of truth may appear a little more ragged and frayed at the edges than the idea of truth that prevailed in the modern age, that may make it all the more compelling.[10]

As a result of this shift from groping after rational proof to seeking to make faithful confessions, Christian preaching becomes a matter of giving public voice to the confessions, convictions, and beliefs of the Christian tradition about what is ultimately and universally true in response to immediate circumstances, all the while never forgetting that these are and remain confessions. The empty tomb, we should keep in mind, in and of itself meant nothing. Rather, what matters was and is the central Easter proclamation that "Christ is risen," a confession of faith that many then and now disputed and disbelieved, yet some believed and, believing, found life in Christ's name. Christian preachers, then, are called to offer their confessions of the truth as clearly, compellingly, and winsomely as possible, confident of their witness yet open to the disagreement and disbelief of others. The responsibility for conversion, from this point of view, rests squarely on the shoulders of the Holy Spirit; the preacher is called only to confess. If we can envision and take up preaching as a practice of confessing, rather than attempting to prove, truth, we will very quickly realize it is a calling that demands equal measures of courage, creativity, and humility. It is a calling that is worthy of all that we have and are.

Telling the Old, Old Story in a New Day

Having sought to describe the essential character of preaching in a postmodern age as confessing the truth of Jesus Christ, we can now move to consider three concrete implications. The first stems from postmodern convictions about the narrative or storied quality of reality: that we all live in, by, and out of some grand narrative that helps us explain everything else (postmodernists also call this a metanarrative or standard story). That is, we make sense of our concrete

10. See Mary McClintock Fulkerson, *Changing the Subject: Women's Discourses and Feminist Theology* (Minneapolis: Fortress Press, 1994), esp. 158–64.

experiences in the world by fitting those experiences into some larger story about the way the world really is. In the modern era, we simply called our narrative "reality," but now we are more keenly aware that different people have very different narratives explaining the world. Some are rooted in religious traditions, and others are secular; some have primarily nationalistic identities, others ethnic. Similarly, we have also realized that there is no objective, neutral court in which to adjudicate which of those multiple narrative constructions is indisputably true. The presence of these differing narratives and our inability to prove rationally the validity of one over all the others has led some postmodern theorists to call for an end to metanarratives. It would be more accurate, however, to say we live in an age of competing metanarratives, of which the Christian story is only one.[11]

In light of this conviction and situation, it is crucial to recognize that in addition to whatever other responsibilities they may have, Christian leaders are, first and foremost, entrusted with telling the Christian story. In this light, we need to reclaim the role of pastoral leaders as "stewards of God's mysteries" (1 Cor. 4:1) in the sense that we are charged with telling the sacred story as vividly and clearly as possible in order to render the Christian narrative as a three-dimensional worldview that seems a viable alternative to our people in light of the other stories, both religious and secular, that they are regularly exposed to.

What response, for example, does the Christian story make to the hyper-consumerism of our culture? From this broad question stems a host of more particular ones: Does Christ's cross and resurrection offer a vision of "abundant life" (John 10:10) that can compete with the "life of abundance" our culture promises is available only through buying and having and owning and consuming ever more? Can families that are harried and hassled by the stresses of work, commuting, and their children's packed schedules to the point of coming apart at the seams expect anything different from the Christian community? In light of the level of poverty in the world and our own nation, can the church offer a different vision than the winner-take-all, survival-of-the-fittest mentality of the marketplace? Does Christ's death and resurrection have anything compelling to say about the meaning of our lives, our work, our relationships, our world, or our future? Does the new life in the Christian community that baptism ushers believers into look and feel any different than

---

11. On the failure of metanarratives, see Jean-François Lyotard's influential work, *The Postmodern Condition: A Report on Knowledge*, trans. Geoff Bennington and Brian Massumi, Theory and History of Literature 10 (Minneapolis: University of Minnesota Press, 1984), 37–41. For a compelling response, see Walter Brueggemann's *Theology of the Old Testament: Testimony, Dispute, Advocacy* (Minneapolis: Fortress Press, 1997), 712.

the competitive rat race so many are caught up in? Joined to Christ's body of believers, what responsibility do we have to those in need?

These are the kinds of questions congregational leaders should be asking and answering—in a variety of venues, but certainly also in and through their sermons—in order to give their hearers the imagination to enter into the biblical narrative and worldview so they might see what life looks like when lived from within the Christian story.

Once again, the Bible intuitively invites us into this task. The obvious but I think incredible thing about the Christian Bible is that it begins at the very beginning in Genesis and ends only at the very end in Revelation, inviting all of us who read and hear it today to imagine ourselves living somewhere between Acts and Revelation. The sermon becomes a primary place where the preacher presents, describes, and explains the Christian story vividly enough that readers can imagine taking their place in that narrative and seeing themselves not only as linked to all the believers who came before them but also as characters in God's ongoing drama to love, bless, and save the world.

A second element of preaching potentially helped by postmodern thought is our view of Scripture and our sense of the power of words. Modernists, you will recall, viewed language as essentially descriptive, the neutral tool by which we describe reality. Postmodernists, in contrast, believe language to be both potent and productive, actually creating and shaping reality rather than merely describing it. In short, words are powerful because they provoke feelings and emotions and actually create the narrative frameworks within which we make sense of the world.

This sense of the productive power of words helps us to reimagine the Bible not primarily as a static repository of religious information about the Christian life but rather as itself a collection of living and active faith claims and assertions about what God has been—and is still!—up to in the world. The Bible, that is, is a collection of confessions that seek a response from whoever reads or hears it. John admits as much at the formal conclusion to his Gospel: "Jesus said and did many other signs that are not written in this book. But these are written that you may believe that Jesus is the Christ, the Son of God, and believing have life in his name" (John 20:30-31). In this brief but telling passage, John reveals not only that he is making creative, authorial decisions in composing his witness ("Jesus did many other signs that are not written in this book; but these are written"), but he also tells us why: "so that you may believe." John, in other words, is after our faith. He offers his confession in order to prompt us to believe the Christian story so we might have life in Christ's name.[12]

All of Scripture is the same; it was not written primarily as a historical document nor as instruction in the religious life, but rather was written by persons who were so gripped by their experience of God's activity in their lives and the world that they had to testify to what they believed God was and is doing in the world. If we can imagine Scripture as this kind of living and active word—indeed, "sharper than any two-edged sword, piercing until it divides soul from spirit, joints from marrow [and] able to judge the thoughts and intentions of the heart" (Heb. 4:12)—then we will be greatly assisted in giving voice to these powerful and provocative confessions in our preaching. Our task is therefore not simply to discover what the passage meant in some historical sense only, nor are we satisfied merely with wondering what Scripture might teach us. Rather, we are looking for what kind of claim the passage of Scripture before us is making on us and our hearers—in other words, what kind of demand, promise, or pledge it contains that will affect our living here and now as we struggle to be the people of God living in mission to and for God's world.

Preaching, then, is a matter of hearing the claims and confessions of Scripture and making them again in our day and age so they can address and affect our hearers with the good news of what God has done and is still doing for us and all the world in and through Jesus the Christ. The words of Scripture, from this postmodern perspective, are less like lead, an inert metal we can work over and shape, than like uranium, alive and pulsing and able to transform whatever is around it. Our job is to open up these powerful words and see what happens.

A third area for our consideration stems from the skepticism postmodernists (and here not just philosophers but also many of our younger members) direct toward received tradition. It's not that postmodernists assume everything handed down to us is wrong; it's more that they balk at being expected to believe it just because, quite frankly, some dead white guy said it was true a hundred, or five hundred, or two thousand years ago. Traditions—whether they are religious, philosophical, or cultural—were conditioned by their particular time and place and corroded by the self-interest of those who originated and now maintain them, so they cannot be trusted for their own sake. Rather, truth must be continually revalidated through experience.

12. Luke makes a similar confession in the opening of his book, where he relates not only that he was not an eyewitness and is therefore dependent on other witnesses but also that he is working with a variety of confessions in order to render one that makes sense ("an orderly account") in order that Theophilus may be confident, or certain, of that in which he has been instructed (Luke 1:14).

This does not mean that one's immediate experience is the only valid standard in some kind of postmodern exercise in narcissism. Rather, it means that for tradition to have validity, it must in some way touch, shape, and fit into our experience. Postmodern hearers, that is, won't simply believe something is true because you say it; rather, they will believe it is true when you say it in a way that rings true to some element of their own experience. In fact, at their best, postmodern hearers, because of their embrace of skepticism, may be willing to have their own beliefs, preconceptions, and convictions challenged by the preacher's words—but only if the preacher first tries to relate his or her message to the actual realities and experiences of the hearer.

This helps illumine the role of theological doctrine in preaching. Too often in the modern pulpit, doctrine was offered as information to be learned, one more thing people had to know and believe (in the sense of cognitive assent) in order to be a Christian. In a postmodern pulpit, doctrine serves to make sense of the hearer's experience. The preacher, therefore, doesn't simply explicate some ancient doctrine and then sit back and wait for the hearer to assent to it. Rather, the preacher, taking the hearer's experience of life in this world seriously, proposes Christian doctrine as a way of making sense of that experience, of offering a larger framework in which to understand and navigate the variety of events in our life in this world.

From this perspective, for instance, one does not preach the incarnation expecting twenty-first-century hearers simply to memorize and assent to fourth-century formulations of the twofold nature of Christ as we find them in the Nicene Creed. Rather, preachers offer the incarnation as a promise and confession that God in Christ has been joined to humanity; that God in Christ therefore knows fully what it means to be one of us; that God in Christ has become completely accessible to us and has drawn near to us; that God in Christ has taken on our lot and our lives that we may be joined through Christ to God and thereby have hope in light of our mortality. The doctrine of the incarnation, ultimately, is not about philosophical or theological formulations but is about what it means to be a human in need of forgiveness and healing, wholeness and salvation, and the lengths and depths to which God will go to bring those to us.

If the Christian faith is, among other things, a grand narrative or worldview that attempts to make sense of all of our lives, then theological doctrines are the signposts and markers along the narrative route. Historically, Christian doctrine was initially proposed and formulated as a means of making sense of the varied experiences Christian communities had of life in Christ as they wrestled with Scripture and with living in the world together. In this sense, doctrine was originally an attempt to order the reflections of Christians on their actual experience of living simultaneously in the world and in Christ. But somewhere along the way, doctrine came to exist for its own sake, demanding to be believed not because of how it informed our actual living and dying but because it had been handed down from church authorities. Such conceptions of doctrine will no longer hold. For those willing to sacrifice a bit of that kind of authority, however, doctrine has the potential, once again, to speak a potent and compelling word that takes our experiences seriously, that makes sense of our lives in the world, and that draws us into life in Christ and community together.

MOVING FORWARD WITH POSTMODERN COURAGE

At the outset of this chapter, I argued that the postmodern age holds more opportunities than threats for those Christians willing to take its claims seriously. In light of the discussion thus far, and as a conclusion to these reflections, let me sum up that confidence in a single sentence: perhaps postmodernity can best be understood as the death of modernist optimism that we can save ourselves.

Modernity, after all, sought to establish the entirely rational, humanistic means by which to understand and harness the structures of nature and the universe in order to subdue these things so as to solve all problems, right all wrongs, and usher in a new era of universal well-being. At the dawn of a new century, we must confess that whatever gains the modern era has brought, there have been tremendous, even globe-threatening failures. The human condition, whatever our technological advances, remains largely unchanged, and we are as wonderful and flawed, hopeful and despairing a creation as ever.

It is my sense and conviction that in the wake left from the death of modernist optimism there has emerged an appreciation and even appetite for mystery, an openness to the divine, and an awareness that we cannot save ourselves but stand in need of mercy, forgiveness, and grace. In this day and age, we have inordinate numbers of people searching for something more meaningful and of greater depth than what they have been offered by the culture at large.

Seasoned by their experience with life's failures and disappointments, however, today's hearers yearn for something other than mere optimism or certainty. Rather, what they long for, I believe, is courage. The kind of courage that does not have to insist on being right but rather is willing to risk its confession and make its wager about God's commitment to this world and then see what happens. The kind of courage that is not paralyzed by a lack of certainty but is willing to throw itself into living, striving, and helping in the meantime.

It is my hope that a generation of preachers will rise up to answer this call and respond to this need by surrendering proof for confession, certainty for faith, and optimism for courage. If we can do that, perhaps we may learn together and once again what it means to live and walk by faith in the grace we have seen, heard, and experienced in and through Jesus Christ our Lord.

2

The Preacher and the Postmodern Bible

Having examined a number of the challenges postmodernism and its relentless skepticism present to contemporary preachers, I want in this chapter to focus on one that has been especially vexing: given the variety of vested interests we each bring to the process of biblical interpretation and proclamation, how do we know what a text really *means*? Or to put it more plainly, how do we know which of its many possible meanings is, if not the right one, at least the best one?

In the postmodern era, a text—whether drawn from the Bible, Shakespeare, or the editorial in the local paper—no longer has a single, identifiable meaning but rather can be interpreted in any number of ways. Meaning, once tied so closely to the author, has escaped such bonds and is no longer a matter of retrieval but rather of active construction such that no one—not the preacher or interpreter or even the author—can say with confidence what a given passage means. A remark once attributed to T. S. Eliot well captures our situation. "When I wrote this poem," Eliot is said to have commented shortly after a poem of his became popular, "only God and I knew what it meant. Now only God knows!"

In short, in the wake of the postmodern onslaught on traditional interpretive methods, establishing a text's "true meaning" has become a dicey venture at best. Such a situation has enormous implications for the life and well-being of the church, as interpreting, applying, and above all else proclaiming the normative text of Christianity has been central to its enterprise from the outset.

In response to this postmodern interpretive mayhem, I want to explore the possibility of reclaiming an old practice of the church called *Sachkritik*. Literally meaning "content criticism," *Sachkritik* invites preachers to identify what they believe and confess is the central theological witness of Scripture and use that as a hermeneutical key. Often distrusted by modern scholars for the penchant of interpreters to flatten the variety of voices in Scripture, such an approach to reading and preaching the Scriptures has in recent years fallen out of favor. But I have wondered whether it is possible to modify this kind of "theological interpretation" so that it does not silence the minority voices either in the Bible or in the congregation. Indeed, I am increasingly persuaded that, used with caution, it may offer us the potential for powerfully reclaiming the biblical witness for the church's use in the postmodern era.

Toward the end of sharing this emerging conviction, this chapter divides into three sections. In the first, I briefly describe the impact of the postmodern movement on biblical studies, giving particular attention to questions about the meaning(s) of a text. In the second section, I outline a proposal for fashioning a postmodern version of *Sachkritik* that I describe as "preaching from the center," which may aid us in our reading and interpreting of Scripture. I conclude in the third section by suggesting several ways by which preachers can employ this approach with care and courage to addresses the postmodern challenge to biblical authority and proclamation while bolstering classic Christian convictions about the Scriptures as a meaningful word from God.

Postmodernity and the Bible

Before we jump into the question of meaning, it may be helpful to remind ourselves of several of the significant contours and attributes of the postmodern age that we explored in more detail in the previous chapter. Chief among these attributes are a resolute anti-foundationalism; a deep wariness of the notion that language is neutral and primarily descriptive; a sense of the constructed, even artificial, nature of reality; a keen distrust of the notion of objective reason; and a profound suspicion of all metanarratives.

What links most of these various elements together, as we took up in the last chapter, is a thoroughgoing skepticism toward the reigning philosophical, religious, political, and economic assumptions about the nature of reality. By naming skepticism as the central attitude of postmodernism, we've also identified the direct, although admittedly ambivalent, relationship it bears to the era it seeks to transcend. For skepticism is by no means foreign to modernity; indeed, in many respects, skepticism was precisely what gave birth to modernity. From Descartes to Freud, the first move of the architects and adherents of modernity was to gaze with unrelenting suspicion on the traditions they inherited. But whereas modern suspicion was always exercised in service to discovering a greater truth, postmodern skepticism operates from the conviction that there is no "greater truth" and that all pretenses to such should be unmasked. Hence, we might say that postmodernity is characterized simultaneously by a frenetic celebration of modernity's skepticism and a marked despair over modernity's optimism—confident, as it were, only in the futility of modernist confidence.

The goal of such a summary rejection of modernity's confidence (and above all, confidence in human reason and progress) is to offer unyielding resistance to the use of power to suppress dissident voices, opinions, and postures in the defense of a homogeneous reality. In this regard, A. K. M. Adam describes postmodernity as a "movement of resistance" against all processes of legitimation, that is, the process of validating something as true, authoritative, and legitimate.[1] While it is tempting at this point to add the modifier "unjust" to this description of what is resisted ("the process of *unjust* legitimation"), doing so drags one into just the kind of quagmire that postmodernists seek to avoid. For who determines between "just" and "unjust" legitimation? And by what standards?

By asking these questions, we have voiced one of the central and unifying tenets of postmodernity: legitimation always implies the (usually tacit) exercise of power. In short, whoever—whether religious, political, or cultural leader—wields the authority to declare what is "true" and what is "false" for a community ultimately holds power within the community. Think about it: when a preacher steps into the pulpit and declares that some practices are "blessed by God" while others are "condemned by God," that's an expression not just of moral discernment but also of power. What makes postmodernists nervous about such pronouncements is precisely that the pronouncements assume one person or group knows beyond a shadow of a doubt what is true or just or blessed, and all others must simply toe the line. It's not that there is no time or place for any moral discernment, but rather the thoughts should be offered as just that: the careful discernment and confession of the one making them, to which others can respond.

Postmodernists, then, are skeptical of processes of legitimation that disguise one particular person's or group's use of power to define the standards (legal, ethical, cultural, religious, philosophical) by which the person or group judges other groups.[2] Hence, Jean-François Lyotard closes his influential article "What Is Postmodernism?" with a call to arms: "Let us wage a war on totality; let us be witnesses to the unpresentable; let us activate the differences and save the honor of the name."[3] Just a decade or so past the bloodiest century in human history,

---

1. A. K. M. Adam, *What Is Postmodern Biblical Criticism?* (Minneapolis: Fortress Press, 1995), 1.

2. This discussion of the relationship between legitimation and power draws from the first chapter of my *Confessing Jesus Christ: Preaching in a Postmodern World* (Grand Rapids, Eerdmans, 1993), esp. pp. 14–15.

and recognizing that much of its bloodshed and violence were carried out in the cause of enforcing one particular version of political, social, or religious "reality," it's difficult not to be at least sympathetic with Lytoard's call.

Postmodernity at its best stands against modernity's penchant to quash dissenting voices in its relentless quest for order, stability, unity, and certainty. At its worst, postmodernity loses all confidence in *any* truth or conviction beyond its own pessimistic views on the absence of truth and the futility of conviction.

It's at just this point that the field of biblical interpretation offers something of a microcosm of the larger postmodern concerns about authority and legitimation. By and large, modern interpreters have assumed that the text means *one* thing, that that "meaning" resides somewhere *in* the text (typically in the intentions of the author) waiting to be discovered, and that, once uncovered, it can be proved, displayed, and ultimately possessed. Hence, modern interpreters committed themselves to the rational-critical, even scientific, road of historical criticism to ascertain the one true approach of a passage with the intent as Friedrich Schleiermacher, one of the architects of "modern theology" optimistically put it, to "understand the intention of the author better than the author himself."[4]

Preaching, following closely on the heels of biblical interpretation, understood its primary purpose in correspondingly clear lines and was, for this reason, a rather straightforward two-step endeavor. First, the preacher figures out and explains what the passage once meant to its original audience (exegesis), and second, the preacher uncovers and shares what the passage should mean for us today (proclamation).

In contrast to modernist interpreters, however, postmodern interpreters assume that "meaning" is not at all univocal or stable, because it is constructed by the reader or community. Therefore, meaning does not resides behind the passage in the author's intention but rather lives and is constructed *in front of* the text, in the interaction between a passage and its readers. Hence, postmodern interpreters are committed to a "multivalent" and "plurivocal" understanding of meaning, employ a variety of methodologies, and assume that the passage

---

3. Jean-François Lyotard, *The Postmodern Condition*, trans. Geoff Bennington and Brian Massumi, Theory and History of Literature 10 (Minneapolis: University of Minnesota Press, 1984), 82.

4. Attributed to Schleiermacher by Hans-Georg Gadamer in *Truth and Method*, trans. and ed. Garrett Barden and John Cumming (New York: Seabury, 1975), 169. More recently, of course, there have been skirmishes over whether literary, structuralist, or canonical criticism (to name just a few) does a better job at distilling the meaning of the text. But the essential confidence in determining the meaning remains the same.

in question can mean any number of things to any number of readers and communities.

In such setting, the two-step waltz danced by so many preachers of an earlier generation begins to falter, as there is no clear consensus about what a given passage might mean or even about how one might attempt to uncover that meaning. As it turns out, in fact, the various exegetical methods we were taught in seminary or have been exposed to since then are *not* simply a collection of neutral instruments in our homiletical toolbox used to decipher the meaning of a passage. Rather, each method represents a distinct and exclusive understanding of *how* a text communicates meaning in the first pace. For this reason, we simply cannot hope to distill a single postmodern method of biblical interpretation, as each method competes with all others as a viable interpretive alternative with its own distinct means by which to determine a text's meaning.

Consider, for example, how various exegetical methods can be distinguished and grouped together in terms of where they locate meaning in the history and composition of a particular text. Source and text criticism, redactor criticism, and all other primarily historical-critical approaches to interpreting a biblical passage assume that the primary location of meaning is *behind* the text (in the historical situation of the composition of the passage). Literary methods, by contrast, stressing the artistic nature of the text and focusing our attention on character development, plot, symbolism, and other literary devices, assert that meaning resides *in* the text. Those who stress the communal and ecclesial nature of the Bible invite us to look at the canonical impulses that drew all these texts together, the history of interpretation, and the church's current use of a passage in the lectionary or immediate church service (wedding, baptism, etc.) and in all these ways urge us to look for meaning *around* the passage in question. Finally, another cluster of interpretive methods gives primary attention to the context and circumstances of the readers and hearers and thereby advocates that we locate meaning *in front of* the text.

Can these various methods complement each other? Certainly, but just as often they offer competing interpretations that cannot be settled by any claim to neutrality, as each method makes a claim as to where meaning is located. Ultimately, methods that were once presented as neutral exegetical tools each turn out to harbor hermeneutical convictions.[5]

---

5. I've written in more detail on this in several places. See "What Does This Mean? A Four-Part Exercise in Reading Mark 9:2-9 (Transfiguration)," in *Word & World* 23, no. 1 (2003): 85–91; and *Confessing Jesus Christ* (Grand Rapids: Eerdmans, 2003), 145–88.

Indeed, what is striking in the current scene of biblical interpretation—and therefore also in preaching—is that there is no convivial dialogue present (the naive postmodern desire and promise) but rather a competitive scramble to locate where meaning resides once and for all. As a result, many preachers awash in the various exegetical methods now available feel as if they are faced with the unsavory choice between insisting on one approach to deciphering the meaning of a biblical passage or surrendering instead to a cacophony of interpretive voices. It is the choice, as one scholar has described it, between the Tower of modernity and the Babel of postmodernity.[6]

This situation has proved nearly disastrous for Christian use of the Bible and for preaching in particular, as it has often bereft preachers of a confident approach to reading and proclaiming the Scriptures and thereby led to what James D. Smart presciently called "the strange silence of the Bible in the Church."[7] In the face of this challenge and need, I am interested in whether it is possible to read the whole of the Bible in light of one's confession of its primary witness. While I don't know whether any single approach can entirely resolve the issues we've named, I believe that reclaiming this overlooked practice of the church might provide a way forward. So it is to the development and testing of this idea that I now turn.

READING SCRIPTURE FROM THE CENTER

The practice of *Sachkritik*—interpreting the whole of Scripture, that is, in light of its central content and witness—has a longer history than some interpreters may recall. For while reading the Bible from the center has most recently been associated with Rudolf Bultmann's work in the middle of the century just past (particularly his commitment to existentialist understandings of "authentic Being"), its presence can be detected in Augustine's interpretative key built around "faith, hope, and love," Luther's focus on justification by grace through faith, and more recent liberation and feminist approaches emphasizing the plight of the poor or marginalized. In short, reading the whole of Scripture in light of its central content attempts to understand discrete passages of Scripture in relation to the core testimony of the biblical witness. That is, it takes what is most clear and central in the Bible as an interpretive lens, or hermeneutic, by which to read all of Scripture. It thereby offers the means to transcend the

---

6. Dennis Olson, "Biblical Theology as Provisional Monologization: A Dialogue with Childs, Brueggemann, and Bakhtin," *Biblical Interpretation* 6 (1998): 171.

7. *The Strange Silence of the Bible in the Church: A Study in Hermeneutics* (Philadelphia: Westminster, 1970).

postmodern interpretive morass by applying a theological, or material, criterion by which to interpret the "meaning" of various passages.

Taking up such an approach is not without peril. Over the years, this kind of "content criticism" has often drawn critical fire for its tendency to determine from the outset the meaning of any and all biblical passages based on a predetermined conclusion about the center of Scripture. Those committed to reading Scripture from the center, critics claim, either twist passages to fit their interpretive mold, ignore passages that don't fit that template, or worst of all, denigrate or even exorcise such passages altogether.[8]

While these criticisms have at times been quite appropriate, I would contend that most of the problems of content criticism arise from the demand (whether modern or premodern) for absolute certainty about the accuracy of one's interpretation. Such certainty was usually acquired through an extreme confidence in either the divine nature of Scripture or the self-evident character of one's hermeneutic (or both!). To reappropriate this ancient practice in our era, one must—with postmodernists—surrender any demand for absolute certitude while simultaneously refusing—with modernists—to despair about the possibility to discern and speak the truth. That is, one must find a middle way that eschews both the Babel and the Tower. In such a pursuit, interpreters will be aided by adopting what I would call an incarnational understanding of Scripture and an intentional and confessional understanding of one's interpretive key to Scripture.

Paul Ricoeur offers significant help in approaching the Bible incarnationally. In his book *Freud and Philosophy*, he takes up the matter of interpretation by distinguishing between two nearly opposite ways to approach a passage. The first, which he calls a hermeneutics of restoration (and is sometimes called a hermeneutic of trust), invites the interpreter to treat the text as a sacred symbol that deserves to be believed completely and unquestioningly. From this point of view, the interpreter reads the text with absolute trust and aims to listen to the passage as closely as possible in order to detect and share the message residing within it. In the second approach, which Ricoeur describes as a hermeneutic of suspicion, the interpreter is far less accepting of the claims of the passage. Realizing that all texts are influenced and even corroded by the historical and cultural biases of their writers, the interpreter brings external critical criteria to bear in order to penetrate beneath the surface meaning of a passage and discover it's "real" meaning.

---

8. Brueggemann, for instance, is wary that any attempt to form a canon within a canon, another phrase for a theological and material criteria, by which to interpret the canon will prove "hegemonic." *Theology of the Old Testament: Testimony, Dispute, Advocacy* (Minneapolis: Fortress Press, 1997), 711.

A number of biblical interpreters since Ricoeur have pitted these two strategies against each other, laying claim to one and criticizing the other. But Ricoeur himself never makes that move. Rather, he advocates employing both a hermeneutic of trust *and* a hermeneutic of suspicion simultaneously. Walter Brueggemann, following Ricoeur, similarly argues that interpretation is more complex than some make out because the whole "life" of a biblical passage—from its composition by an author, its interpretation through history, right up to its reception by contemporary readers—is what he describes as "a mixture of faith and vested interest." Indeed, this is what makes interpretation necessary . . . and also challenging and at times frustrating. As he writes,

> To study "the social process" is to pay attention to this vexed combination. That the textual process is skewed by interest requires a hermeneutic of suspicion. That the textual process is an act of serious faith permits a hermeneutics of retrieval. Despite the identification of these two hermeneutics, the matter remains complicated and problematic because we cannot practice one hermeneutic and then the other. We cannot first sort out vested interest and then affirm faith, because vested interest and faith always come together and cannot be so nicely distinguished. We must simply recognize that the two always come together, even in the midst of our best efforts of discernment and criticism.[9]

The Christian interpreter, in other words, simultaneously trusts that God speaks through the biblical witness even while recognizing that God's speech comes through humans and therefore is always distorted by human sin.[10]

It is precisely by admitting and naming the dual character of Scripture—both entrusted to humans yet accomplishing divine purposes—that the preacher can approach Scripture incarnationally. Further, the hermeneutic of restoration that Ricoeur describes is built around the material criteria, or interpretive center, of Scripture that *Sachkritik* assumes. In other words, one's interpretive key is precisely one's sense of God's most *clear* word–Christ, the living word–in the midst of faithful, yet sinful, human speech.

In this regard, it may be helpful to recall the Reformers' insistence of "Christ over canon," that is, that Christians invariably read the whole of Scripture in light of the confession that the crucified Jesus of Nazareth is also

---

9. Walter Brueggemann, "The Social Nature of the Biblical Text," in *Preaching as a Social Act: Theology and Practice*, ed. Arthur Van Seeters (Nashville: Abingdon, 1988) 131.

10. See also *Confessing Jesus Christ*, 138–43.

the resurrected Christ. Hence, for the Reformers, the cry that we are "justified by grace through faith" wasn't simply a theological confession, it was also a hermeneutical principle, guiding the preacher to look at every passage with regard to how it demonstrates God's commitment to "justify the ungodly" by faith in Christ.

But let's not mislead ourselves by pointing only to the Reformers. As I mentioned previously, it's not difficult to detect a similar impulse in interpreters throughout history. And, I would argue, the habit of developing a "canon within a canon"—understood not as privileging certain books but as reading all of the Bible through one's conviction of its central and primary witness—is evident in all of us who preach and teach. Indeed, give me six months of the sermons of any preacher, and I'll give you a clear and succinct statement of his or her primary theological convictions.

But what about the criticism often leveled at those who intentionally employ such a method? Are we doomed to trumping, whether consciously or unconsciously, the distinct and varied witness of Scripture with our theological criteria? Or to make the matter more personal, must I as a Lutheran preacher make sure every sermon leads to the conviction of sin and the promise of forgiveness (a narrow but prevalent understanding of "law and gospel")? Similarly, must a Methodist sermon always lead to instruction about sanctification, a Mennonite sermon discuss peace, or an Episcopal sermon always refer to the Eucharist? Does Scripture, in other words, have nothing more to say to us than what we have already heard and perceived?

These are important questions. To address them, and in this way to avoid the pitfalls inherent in a modernist approach to interpreting from the center, preachers and other interpreters must make two interrelated moves. First, they must intentionally make the hermeneutical criteria they employ as explicit as possible, and second, they must regard these criteria as a confession of faith rather than a self-evident, rationally demonstrable, and timeless truth.

By intentionally describing our interpretive criteria, we invite others into a dialogue, not only about the results of our study, but also about the premises and presuppositions of our study itself. This means, among other things, that criteria that differ from our own can never be silenced or ruled immediately out of bounds. Conversely, it also means that our own criteria can never be removed from the pale of critical review, revision, and even reversal. By making our convictions about Scripture's core witness evident, we invite others into a meaningful, dynamic, and ongoing conversation about what we believe is at the very heart of Scripture. Conducted carefully and regularly, such a conversation will not only lead to keeping the preacher "honest" (as the voices of other members of the community can more easily point out some of our unconscious biases or presuppositions), but it will also invite our hearers and partners to think more holistically about what Scripture has to say to them and to our world.

To enter into this conversation, we not only need to be intentionally honest about our convictions, but must also name them as such. That is, we must confess what we believe to be at the heart of the biblical witness, rather than attempting to prove it once and for all. By confessing one's interpretive center, interpreters and preachers avoid the totalizing and aggressive penchant of modern interpretation, where every differing interpretation is a rival for the one, true approach. At the same time, confessing one's hermeneutical assumptions allows preachers to retain the strength of their convictions, thus avoiding the despair and confusion of postmodern interpretation, where every interpretation is equally a matter of self-projection.

This kind of vulnerable disclosure (for confessing, rather than proving, one's position always entails the possibility for disagreement and rejection) not only provides a key to reclaiming a vibrant understanding of interpretation but also invites a more communal and conversational approach to the task of proclamation. In this last section, I will suggest some of the primary advantages and possibilities such an approach offers.

Preaching the Postmodern Bible

The approach I've suggested—inviting a postmodern twist on the classic understanding of *Sachkritik*—offers a path through the postmodern tumult of competing interpretations without raising the preacher above all other readers of Scripture in the congregation. To explore further some of the potential of this approach, I will describe briefly eight possibilities it holds for today's preachers.

1. Preaching the Bible from the center simultaneously allows room for, and holds accountable, the ineluctable role of our own biases, vested interests, and predispositions. One of the targets of postmodern critique has been modernity's projection of the "objective" character of rational-critical research. A postmodern version of content criticism not only allows for the inevitability of the subjective but honors it. As Bultmann demonstrated decades ago, not only is it impossible to study and interpret texts without some level of self-involvement, but to attempt to eliminate the subjective through some "neutral" method is only to fall prey to the biases inherent in that method.[11] While honoring the subjective,

---

11. See *Jesus and the Word*, trans. Louise Pettibone Smith and Erminie Huntress Lantero (New York: Charles Scribner's Sons, 1962 [1934]), esp. 3–15; and "Is Exegesis without Presuppositions Possible?,"

however, a postmodern approach to reading the Bible from the center also holds it accountable, not by neutralizing one's confession about what constitutes the center but rather by making it explicit and therefore placing it in a larger conversation where others can acknowledge and critique it.

To put that another way, we preachers do not come to Scripture without a set of questions influenced by our context and experience. And we should not, as our questions are what bring us to the text in the first place. At the same time, by admitting that our context and experience powerfully shape not only our questions *for* Scripture but also our expectations *of* Scripture, we make room for others—including the voices within the Scriptures—to call into question our questions, both keeping us honest and keeping a vibrant conversation going.

2. Reading and preaching the Bible from the center avoids the fragmentation of the biblical witness into a series of discrete parts. Though historical-critical method has greatly enhanced our knowledge of the many sources that contribute to various books or parts of the Bible, (J, E, D, P, etc.), it has also seriously injured our sense of the integrity of the biblical witness. But by approaching the Bible as a complete book united by a common theme and witness, rather than as a happenstance collection of independent and often irreconcilable parts, preachers can better help their people enter into the biblical drama.

We do this in part by preaching from the Bible, rather than from "the author we name Luke," "proto-Mark," "the final redactor of John," or other such constructions that, while perhaps useful for understanding the background of a passage, continue to heighten confusion about how the various parts of the Bible hold together. Indeed, cultivating a lively sense of the "heart of the biblical witness" provides a way to draw hearers consistently back to the narrative arc of God's loving intention and saving activity through the long and varied story of the Bible.

Will some passages diverge from or even contradict one's conviction about the primary content of the Bible (in my case just described as "God's loving intention and saving activity")? Absolutely, but when we confess our hermeneutical proposals as, in fact, proposals, divergent passages—and the people reading them—can stretch, strengthen, or correct our proposals even while deepening the community's confidence in reading and living the biblical witness.

3. Preaching the Bible from the center reminds us that our interpretations, along with all of language, are productive and even powerful, rather than merely descriptive.

Existence and Faith: Shorter Writings of Rudolf Bultmann, trans. Schubert M. Ogden (Cleveland: World, 1960), 289–96.

We are not, ultimately, called as preachers to discover the one, true, and final meaning of a passage, but rather to offer a lively and compelling interpretation of it that speaks to the immediate situation of our community of hearers and actually has an effect on them. By and large, preachers have been trained in their interpretation to give particular attention to the *past* of a given passage of Scripture, whether seeking to understand the author's intention, its place in the canon, or its use and interpretation in the history of the church. *Sachkritik*, however, calls for a present-tense confession of our communal convictions about God and the central witness of Scripture and its immediate import. So while the past still matters, preaching the Bible from the center invites us to be equally—indeed, to be more—interested in the *present* and *future* of a passage. Certainly we take seriously where a text has come from and how it has been read in the past, but our central call is to give careful voice to what this passage may mean and do to present-day hearers. Hence, our primary question when approaching a passage is not "Where did it come from?" or "What did it mean?" but rather "What might it do to the community that gathers around it when next heard?"

This postmodern focus on the ability of language not just to *say* something but to *do* something has important implications for preaching. For just as our preoccupation with the various and sundry compositional elements of the Bible (J, proto-Mark, etc.) can split the whole into a loose collection of variously related parts, so also can it turn interpretation into an intellectual affair and distance hearers from any meaningful engagement with their book. Mark Allan Powell has demonstrated convincingly that while preachers come to the text with a primary goal of understanding what a passage "means" (meaning as cognitive explanation), hearers are far more interested in what the passage "means for me" (meaning as emotional effect).[12] Postmodernity's conviction about the dynamism of language, including the language of our preached interpretations, invites us to focus not just on what the words of Scripture once meant, but on what they may mean and do to our hearers today and in the days to come.

4. *A postmodern practice of reading and preaching from the center stresses a corporate, rather than individualistic, approach to Scripture.* In modernity, exegetical study and proclamation has been all too often an individual affair, with a lone preacher digging through a text in search of its meaning in order to display it to the congregation during the Sunday-morning sermon. But theological criteria

---

12. Mark Allan Powell, *What Do They Hear? Bridging the Gap between Pulpit and Pew* (Nashville: Abingdon, 2007), 65ff.

arise far more often from the historic and present-day community's corporate worship and study. Meaning making, whether we understood it this way or not, has always been inherently communal. And if we can preach in a way that lifts up our core convictions while simultaneously inviting people to share theirs, we might be able to extend the preaching moment beyond the time spent in the pulpit. We might even invite people into our preparation of the sermon by tending an ongoing conversation about the meaning of the passages on which we are preaching.

In recent years, several homileticians have given significant and salutary thought to how we can engage our hearers in this kind of communal meaning making, which at its best is exactly what interpretation and preaching should be.[13] Whether through study of the passage ahead of time or participation in the sermon itself, there is an increasing number of ways by which to make proclamation a more shared endeavor. Be prepared: this kind of freer-flowing and more communal interpretation will definitely bring to light differences in interpretation. But by confessing one's interpretive criteria up front and by holding one's conclusions more loosely as faithful confessions rather than as scientific proofs, the preacher can serve as host and facilitator of the community's ongoing and holy dialogue about the faith and can nurture a meaningful conversation of convictions rather than simply mediate a confrontation between opposing points of view.

5. *This emphasis on the communal nature of hermeneutical criteria invites us to a broader vision of "meaning" itself.* The postmodern turn in biblical studies reminds us—indeed, insists—that there is no *one* meaning. Rather, communities of faith shape meaning in relation to their context, history, and deeply held convictions. Judiciously employing a postmodern version of content criticism can aid communities in identifying what matters to them, help them understand their interpretations, and open them to being stretched and challenged by dissonant readings from voices within or outside the community.

A question often arises, however, in conversations about reading and preaching the Bible from the center, as well as from the postmodern condition more generally: Is openness to a biblical passage having multiple meanings the same as saying a biblical passage can mean anything? Powell, again, is helpful as he invites multiple valid readings of a passage so long as each is grounded in the particular details of the text. The key is to trust the passage in question

---

13. See, for instance, John McClure, *The Roundtable Pulpit: Where Preaching and Leadership Meet* (Nashville: Abingdon, 1997); Lucy Atkinson Rose, *Sharing the Word: Preaching in the Roundtable Church* (Louisville: Westminster John Knox, 1997); and Doug Pagitt, *Preaching in the Inventive Age* (Minneapolis: Sparkhouse, 2011).

to place boundaries around the community's interpretation even as it provides significant freedom in interpretation.[14]

6. If interpretation is communal, it will also be contested. Communities, even relatively homogeneous communities, are rarely univocal, so they will sometimes experience sharp differences in interpretation. By carefully and publicly cultivating the practice of preaching the Bible from the center, however, preachers can shift debates over contested issues from the exegetical to the hermeneutical level.

That is, ultimately we are more interested in how we read the Bible than simply in what we find there while reading. Strikingly, it is difficult to find one significant issue debated in the church, theological or social, that was settled at the exegetical level. From debates over Christology and the sacraments in the fourth and sixteenth centuries, to those over slavery and the ordination of women in the nineteenth and twentieth, to those about human sexuality most recently, the data culled from careful exegetical study was far more frequently what *elicited* the problem than what solved it. For instance, it was precisely a close reading of both John's understanding of the preexistent and eternal Word (John 1) and Luke's confession that Jesus grew in stature and wisdom (Luke 2) that prompted the Christological controversy. Similarly, breakthroughs to such exegetical "inconsistencies" and the theological logjams they occasioned occurred only when one hermeneutical approach (what else is the Chalcedonian formula but a map for reading divergent passages of Scripture?) was accepted by disputing parties—or perhaps simply triumphed over time.

Differences of opinion and even controversy are, I think, inevitable among committed Christians trying to apply a two-thousand-year-old book to current issues and concerns. Preaching the Bible from a confessed center, however, becomes a helpful reminder to us amid our immediate concerns that we do better to resist the temptation to settle our differences by shooting each other with "Bible bullets" we've culled from supposedly neutral exegesis and instead move the discussion to our hermeneutical presuppositions about what is at the heart of Scripture. While this is not meant to undermine careful exegetical work (the source of our hermeneutical convictions), it *is* intended to remind us that by being honest about our deepest convictions about the nature and

---

14. In a stunning example of this "interpretive freedom within textual boundaries" drawn from his own experience, Powell describes three quite different readings of the Prodigal Son by interpreters in the United States, Russia, and Africa. Each reflects close attention to the passage as well as to the culture, context, and experience of the community of interpretation. *What Do They Hear?*, 11ff.

intent of God—convictions that shape our reading of all the varied passages in Scripture—we might invite others to meet us on such ground.

7. *Reading and preaching the Bible from the center preserves Scripture's status as the divine word of God even while taking seriously the "incarnational" element of Scripture's composition, transmission, reception, and interpretation by fallible humans.* By taking both the human dimension and divine intention of Scripture with equal seriousness, we can invite our hearers to imagine how they are also invited to give witness in this day and age. That is, by noticing that the Bible's various writers (not to mentioned characters!) were imperfect in their witness yet were used by God, we might be able to imagine more easily that God also seeks to use the imperfect witnesses of our time and community to give powerful testimony to God's divine intention to love, bless, and save all the world. We might, that is, see ourselves not as standing so far apart from these earlier Christians but imagine ourselves as the latest in a long line of witnesses.

8. *This approach to biblical interpretation gives the preacher something to say with conviction.* While we may offer our interpretations humbly enough to allow others to disagree (an appropriate response to the eschatological nature of the gospel), yet we speak because we believe that what we say is true. Further, we recognize that real dialogue stems only from the mutual confession of one's convictions. Hence, our interpretations are simultaneously tentative and bold, humble and confident, made always and only by faith in the promises of the living God.

Preaching, from this point of view, is meant to be provocative, eliciting conversation and questions, faith or disbelief, but always striving to make a claim worth responding to. In this way, the preacher comes not as the trained expert designated to give a guided tour of an ancient text—let alone perform a postmortem on a dead confession of faith—but rather as an experienced guide and host who makes claims, suggests lively interpretations, makes a wager about the present-day meaning and interpretation of a passage, and ultimately, invites the hearer not just to take these claims and confessions seriously but also to respond to them in word and deed.

As I suggested at the outset of this chapter, the "death of meaning" has haunted much biblical interpretation in the postmodern era, often drawing preachers and other Christian leaders into an unfortunate either/or sense that a passage must mean one thing or anything. But I think reading and preaching the Bible from the center—what I have sometimes called a postmodern version of *Sachkritik*—helps us to take seriously both the challenges and the opportunities of the postmodern era while eschewing its penchant for nihilism. It advocates against the quest for indisputable certainty of modernity and the despair and eventual silence of postmodernity. In this way, it suggests a different sense of meaning, one that is confessed rather than possessed, one that is located within imperfect communities nevertheless fashioned by the Word, and one that can be spoken truthfully and powerfully if not proved undeniably true.

Let me again reiterate that there is certainly no one way to read and preach Scripture in the postmodern era, and this postmodern emphasis on identifying a central and unifying interpretive core to Scripture will undoubtedly work better with some passages and for some communities than with others. While granting its limitations, however, I nevertheless believe that such an approach—confessing one's sense of the gospel and allowing this to shape all of our reading—forces us, among other things, to trust in God for our final vindication, to respect others in the meantime, and in both of these ways to learn once again to live by faith alone. Further, I am convinced that we have little choice in the matter. This side of the eschaton, we cannot perfectly discern the one, true "meaning" of all Scripture but rather, like Moses, often can see only the trail of God's passing through the biblical witness and attempt to follow that trail as faithfully as we are able.

On any given Saturday night, as the preacher labors away, wrestling a sermon from the appointed biblical reading, that may not seem like much. But come Sunday morning, if the preacher has the nerve to climb once more into the pulpit to give voice to how this distinct passage gives witness to the heart of the God we discover across the pages of Scripture, it more often than not proves to be enough.

PART II

Secularism

3

Preaching Hope in the Secular Age

SECULARISM AND THE LOSS OF THE TRANSCENDENT

There's a scene in the film adaptation of Suzanne Collins's dystopian novel *The Hunger Games* that, while it wasn't in the book, fits the story perfectly. President Snow, the totalitarian ruler of futuristic Panem, asks his chief Games-maker—the one charged with creating a spectacle as entertaining as it is barbaric—why the Games must have a winner. The answer? Hope. Snow wants to give the oppressed people of Panem hope that maybe, just maybe, the odds will be in their favor and they may win the Hunger Games and escape their life of servitude. "Hope," he explains, "is the only thing more powerful than fear." But for that very reason, it is as perilous to a dictator as it is useful: "A little hope," he explains, "is effective; a lot of hope is dangerous."

I raise at the outset of this chapter the question of hope because that is the one thing I notice most often missing from conversations about the present state of the church. Longstanding members of our congregations bemoan declines in attendance in general and grieve the absence of their children and grandchildren in particular. Leaders wonder what they have done wrong even as they struggle with fatigue from the monstrous hours they put in trying to revive stagnant congregations. There is, among our churches and people, a pervasive lack of hope regarding the future of the Christian tradition in these lands.

Whether they know it or not, the loss of hope so many of our people and leaders express is a characteristic not just of the church but of the larger secular age in which the church exists. For if, as we've already discussed, postmodernity represents a loss of confidence in modernity's optimism about human reason and progress, secularism represents a loss of confidence not in human things, but divine. As Harvey Cox writes in his seminal *The Secular City*, secularization is characterized by "the discovery by man that he has been left with the world on his hands, that he can no longer blame fortune or the furies for what he does with it. Secularization is man turning his attention away from worlds beyond and toward this world and time."[1] The result of this "discovery" has resulted in a kind of "shrinking" of the cosmos, a recognition that the more we explore, the more we find that there is nothing "out there" that will save us. We are on our own.

Secularism, therefore, urges us to look not outward for hope and meaning, but inward toward the quest of human fulfillment and flourishing. As Charles Taylor describes in his monumental *A Secular Age*, secularism represents the triumph of the immanent over the transcendent.[2] But that triumph has come with a cost. Absent any confidence that a transcendent order undergirds our efforts, beliefs, and very lives, much of life seems flat, even superficial. As Taylor writes, "How to describe this sense? Perhaps in terms like this: our actions, goals, achievements, and the like, have a lack of weight, gravity, thickness, substance. There is a deeper resonance which they lack, which we feel should be there."[3]

Viewed this way, secularism is a condition in which both the religious and nonreligious find themselves struggling for hope. For far from being antagonistic to religion, secularism—born of modernity's interest in separating faith and reason and accelerated by postmodernity's acknowledgment of epistemological relativism—is more aptly described as *post*-religious. It's not that religious faith claims don't matter or have been invalidated; rather, the function of religious claims to provide a coherent, meaningful, and explanatory narrative about the world has been replaced by other, more material stories.[4]

In response to this loss of confidence in a transcendent reality, some assert their faith claims more aggressively than ever (fundamentalism), others make their claims more tentatively and with attention to the validity of other traditions (mainline progressive), while still others surrender them altogether—some slowly and with grief (agnostics), others with gleeful abandon (atheists). But all these reactions are symptoms of the same secular awareness that in Western cultures, belief in the transcendent has receded, replaced by material and economic stories that, a decade into the twenty-first century, we now realize have failed to provide a satisfyingly meaningful narrative.

Viewed this way, the mainline decline so many of us have observed with equal measures of horror and helplessness makes far more sense. It's not that

---

1. Harvey Cox, *The Secular City: Secularization and Urbanization in Theological Perspective* (New York: Macmillan, 1965), 2.

2. Taylor, *A Secular Age* (Cambridge, MA: The Belknap Press of Harvard University Press, 2007), 21.

3. Ibid., 307.

4. See F. S. Michaels, *Monoculture: How One Story Is Changing Everything* (Red Clover, 2011). See also Cox, *The Secular City*, 2–3.

faith doesn't matter to our people, it's more that it no longer plays as meaningful a role as it did for our parents in helping us navigate our day-to-day lives in a secular world. For when transcendence has been banished to the personal and private dimensions of our lives, God, as Walter Brueggemann puts it, no longer functions as a primary character in the narrative of our lives.[5] Church attendance correspondingly becomes more a matter of tradition and obligation and, over time, is replaced by other activities related to work and family that, while they may do no better of a job offering a palpable sense of meaning and purpose, at least demonstrate their pragmatic value more readily.

Nor is it just the mainline that's in trouble anymore. According to a 2012 report by the Hartford Institute for Religion Research, all major Christian traditions in North America declined during the 2000s. Hence, just a decade into the twenty-first century, all Christians, from liberal to conservative, Baptist to Brethren, Roman Catholic to Protestant, and fundamentalist to mainline, appear now to be in the same secularist boat—and it seems to be sinking fast.

This may seem a fairly somber assessment of the current state of the church in a post-religious, post-transcendent secular age. I offer it for three reasons. First, I suspect that, as much as it may pain us, most of us would agree that the Christian church and its witness in these lands are in dire straits. But while this recognition can lead to either rabid retrenchment or unhelpful nostalgia, it can also sound an alarm to action, calling us to do something. The question, of course, is what should we be doing? While there is no easy answer to this question, it helps, I believe, to at least be asking the *right* question. Indeed, I would suggest, as Diana Butler Bass urges, that wrestling with the question of what Christianity may look like in a world that has lost its religion is the central issue of our age.[6]

Second, recognizing the secular crisis in front of us also offers us a caution. The typical reaction of many organizations in crisis is to look inward, to become preoccupied if not obsessed with the need to survive, and to organize most of their efforts toward staving off their own demise. Operating in a reactive posture, institutions lose the creative energy to offer hope of new possibilities because they themselves have lost the imagination to see beyond the patterns and practices that have served them to this point but are manifestly no longer adequate.[7]

---

5. Walter Brueggemann, *The Practice of Prophetic Imagination: Preaching an Emancipating Word* (Minneapolis: Fortress Press, 2012), 2–4.

6. Diana Butler Bass, *Christianity after Religion: The End of Church and the Birth of a New Spiritual Awakening* (San Francisco: HarperOne, 2012).

Most of us know what this feels like. Whether it's a local congregation cutting its outreach, benevolence, and education programs in order to pay its heating bills, or whether it's a national church body obsessing over internal theological, moral, and ecclesial regulations and controversies rather than reaching out to the unchurched, the poor, and all those in need of the good news of the gospel, this tendency to become self-absorbed out of a concern for survival is as natural as it is destructive. But it is also, I would argue, antithetical to the gospel message, a message that does not promise unending life, let alone success, but rather promises resurrection from the dead. For this reason, in this time of significant crisis and opportunity, we must look not inward but outward. Instead of asking, "What do *we* need?" we must ask the far more biblical question, "What does my neighbor need, what does my community need, what does the world need?" so that we might give ourselves, spend ourselves, for the sake of the world God loves so much.

The third and final reason to explore candidly and briefly the impact the secular age has had on the lives of our faith communities is simply that unless we get the diagnosis of our condition correct, we cannot hope to offer a fit prescription. Taking seriously the recognition of Taylor, Cox, and others that secularism is characterized most directly by a loss of a sense of transcendence, we realize that one of the primary challenges of the age is that we, both inside the church and out, have lost hope—hope that there is something more than meets the eye, hope that some values exist beyond those we can construct, hope that our actions and lives are rooted in a larger framework of meaning. While some greet this loss of hope with a sober acceptance, inviting what they describe as a more realistic and courageous response to an impartial and unfeeling universe, most find that the dissolution of a transcendent narrative robs them of significant joy and purpose.

I believe this is a challenge well suited to Christianity, as the birth of the Jesus movement stems from the at-first astonished and then somewhat fearful but ultimately hope-filled confession that "Jesus is risen." For what else is the proclamation of resurrection but a declaration of faith in a transcendent reality?

The difficulty, however, is that as children of our secular, postmodern world, we have grown suspicious that *any* narrative, sacred or secular, suffices to provide meaning adequate to the demands of the day. To put it another way, it's not that we question the importance of the faith passed down to us from our parents, it's more that we aren't sure it is relevant to our complex

---

7. On the "reactive zone" or phase in church life, see Alan Roxburgh and Fred Romanuk, *The Missional Leader: Equipping Your Church to Reach a Changing World* (San Francisco: Jossey-Bass, 2006), 37–60.

and largely material lives. So if postmodernity challenges us to explore the possibility for claiming the Christian story is *true*, secularism demands to know how Christianity is *relevant*.

The question of Christianity's credibility and relevance isn't, of course, novel. For the last two centuries at least, the Christian faith has increasingly struggled to offer as complete and comprehensive an explanation for the way the world works as does the rational and mechanistic worldview ushered in by the Enlightenment. As scientific progress grew, it seemed, the purview and importance of religious faith shrank, relegated to the private and personal dimensions of our life.

But as we've begun to reconsider the benefits and costs of the rationalistic, scientific worldview we so optimistically adopted, the opportunity presents itself to look at Christianity not as a competing explanation for how the world works, but rather as a generative narrative as to *why* it works. In this sense, we are invited to see Christianity as one answer to the distinctively secular question of whether our life has meaning, purpose, and hope. Christianity becomes relevant, that is, precisely as it responds to the secular crisis of hope. For it to do so effectively, however, I believe we need to abandon the ambition we've pursued since the dawn of the Enlightenment of fitting Christianity into modernity's mechanistic worldview in the hope of making it rationally credible. In fact, I think we instead need to embrace precisely the more transcendent elements of its story and claims in order to speak to a world rich in credibility but poor in mystery and hope.

Outlining how Christianity might rise to this challenge posed by a world that is as secular as it is postmodern will take up the remainder of this chapter and the next. In this chapter, I will make a theological argument that the key to offering a compelling witness to the transcendent hope at the heart of Christianity rests in reclaiming the distinctive character of the story in which that hope is rooted. In the next, I will address the vital and pragmatic question of whether our lives hold meaning beyond what we can assign to them. For this reason, this chapter will be somewhat more broadly thematic in character as I explore two significant dimensions of the hope we proclaim: First, Christian hope resides outside of ourselves in the activity of a transcendent God. And second, Christian hope is the "impossible possibility" announced, not proved, in Scripture.

Resurrection Hope

In 1948, in a world overshadowed by the horror of World War II, a world ravaged by the effects of that war, a world still reeling from its encounter with evil manifested in the deaths of millions of children and women and men, a group of Dominican monks invited the famous philosopher and atheist Albert Camus to tell them what non-Christians expected of Christians in our common life together. Camus, one of those who most celebrated the decline of the transcendent in public life, offered a response that was tellingly brief. Absent a shared larger narrative about God and the world, he focused instead on a shared commitment to achieving a more moral world by urging his hearers to join him, as he writes, in "interced[ing] almost everywhere and ceaselessly for children and for [adults]."[8]

His response is not only brief; it is also painfully realistic, as he acknowledges how small, even pathetic, the efforts of moral persons can be. So he ends up pleading with his hearers that if they cannot defeat evil, at least they combat it: "Perhaps we cannot prevent this world from being a world in which children are tortured," he admits. "But we can reduce the number of tortured children. And if you don't help us, who else in the world can help us?"[9]

Interestingly, however, after making this meager plea, Camus moves on to identify something Christians can offer that he himself cannot. In doing so, he puts his finger, I think, on the defining characteristic of Christianity and our best offering to the secular world. Camus confesses that he cannot "pass myself off as a Christian. . . . [For while] I share with you the same revulsion of evil . . . . I do not share your hope."[10]

And there it is in a nutshell: the one distinctive thing Christians have to offer this most secular of worlds: hope. This hope, let me be clear, is not merely optimism. For while some preachers across the centuries (and certainly in our own day) have peddled optimism and success as the heart of the Christian gospel, we cannot afford to be fooled by such a distortion. While optimism involves the expectation that things are eventually going to get better, hope asserts that no matter what may come, no matter how bad things may get, yet God's word and promise will prevail.

Further, and just as importantly, the hope to which we bear witness is born not of our own accomplishments, abilities, or prospects, but rather is founded upon the activity of God in Jesus Christ, and particularly God's activity

8. Albert Camus, "The Unbeliever and Christians," in *Resistance, Rebellion, and Death: Essays* (New York: Vintage, 1996), 70.

9. Ibid., 69.

10. Ibid., 71.

hidden in the cross and resurrection. Consider, for instance, the witness of the apostle Paul. Writing to his stubborn, independent, fractious, and skeptical congregation in Corinth, Paul writes the following response to questions they posed about the resurrection:

> Now if Christ is proclaimed as raised from the dead, how can some of you say there is no resurrection of the dead? If there is no resurrection of the dead, then Christ has not been raised; and if Christ has not been raised, then our proclamation has been in vain and your faith has been in vain. We are even found to be misrepresenting God, because we testified of God that he raised Christ—whom he did not raise if it is true that the dead are not raised. For if the dead are not raised, then Christ has not been raised. If Christ has not been raised, your faith is futile and you are still in your sins. Then those also who have died in Christ have perished. If for this life only we have hoped in Christ, we are of all people most to be pitied. But in fact Christ has been raised from the dead, the first fruits of those who have died. (1 Cor. 15:12-20)

Note, in regard to our question about the locus of hope, the clarity, realism, and courage that permeate Paul's Letter to the Corinthians and that matches anything Camus has to offer. "If Christ has not been raised," Paul writes, "then our proclamation has been in vain and your faith is in vain."

Paul recognizes that, taken at face value, his ministry to the church at Corinth *cannot* validate itself. That is, there is nothing available for Paul or the Corinthians with which to anchor their sense of security or confidence in what they themselves can do. It doesn't matter what a great preacher Paul is, it doesn't matter how lively or vivacious Corinthian worship is, it doesn't matter that the church was growing by leaps and bounds or how many people spoke in tongues. None of this can guarantee the validity of their faith. For this reason, unless Paul looks to God's activity in the resurrection of Christ—this event outside of his own accomplishments and experience—he simply cannot tell whether his own preaching and ministry, his own faith and the faith of his parishioners, have been anything but futile.

The same is true for us: nothing in our immediate, subjective experience, in and of itself, can validate either our faith or our ministry. Such a statement would have been impossible to make during the reign of modernity, where our immediate experience, moved from subjective to objective via scientific analysis, forms the entirety of our reality. But in a postmodern world, we are invited to look beyond ourselves, questioning the lack of transcendence that has both defined and crippled secularism. Hence, hearkening back to the premodern apostle, to find this kind of confidence, courage, and hope, we look elsewhere, clinging to Christ's cross and resurrection.

When we embrace the confession that God appears where we least expect God to be in order to create light from darkness and give life to the dead, we find two vital things happen. First, we discover that we are free. How so? Because we're already dead. If the cross means nothing else, you see, it certainly means there is an end to the physical life and a limitation to physical ability. In this regard, those secularists who celebrate the loss of the transcendent as a call for courage are right. For no matter what our accomplishments or successes, our possessions or attainments, we are joined to all other people in that we are ultimately vulnerable, fragile—in a word, mortal—and therefore born to die. Or to put it more bluntly, if life is the goal of life, then we are born failures.

But it is precisely for this reason—precisely because we *are* doomed to failure and death, and have, in fact, already died in baptism—that we can no longer be discouraged by the fear of failure or death (Rom. 6:1-4). For those who are doomed to fail are the freest persons in the world. And those who are dead have nothing left to fear, and nothing to lose. Camus knew this as well as any. Consider Dr. Rieux, chief protagonist of *The Plague*, who faces undaunted the devastating illness ravaging his community. Knowing he is about to die, he has a choice: he can deny or flee that death, or he can embrace it and discover the courage to stand against it in utter and hopeless freedom.

Contrast the brave hopelessness of the fictional Dr. Rieux, however, with the actual words of Martin Luther King Jr., who on the evening preceding his own encounter with mortality sensed the gravity of the moment and claimed a different kind of freedom, the freedom that was his in Christ. After taking his hearers on a brief tour of history, stopping at a number of the high points of human achievement, Dr. King confessed that he would rather live at no other time than this one, when the promise of freedom was on the verge of being extended to more people than ever before. Not that it had been achieved. No, there was, he acknowledged, still a long way to go. But on that night in Memphis, Dr. King was at peace. As he told the crowd that had come out to hear him,

> Like anybody, I would like to live a long life. Longevity has its place.
> But I'm not concerned about that now. I just want to do God's will.
> And He's allowed me to go up to the mountain. And I've looked
> over. And I've seen the Promised Land. I may not get there with you.

> But I want you to know tonight, that we, as a people, will get to the promised land! And so I'm happy, tonight. I'm not worried about anything. I'm not fearing any man! Mine eyes have seen the glory of the coming of the Lord!!

Having been to the mountaintop and having looked over and seen the promised land, King was able to say he had no more fear. He was, like Camus's Dr. Rieux, free.

Moreover, it is the freedom Paul promises also to us. Paul asserts, in fact, that because we have died in Christ, we are free to thrust ourselves entirely into the challenges all around us. We are, in this sense, like a terminally ill patient who, having accepted her fate, thrusts herself into life, determined to suck from it all the juices it has left for her. Or, to refer once again to Camus, we are like the doctor in a town ravaged by the plague, free to spend ourselves standing against the abyss with hopeless courage and reckless abandon.

But make no mistake: the similarity ends here. Note that King's freedom is a hopeful, rather than desperate, freedom because it is rooted not in what we can accomplish on our own but in God's promise to redeem all things. So far from bearing the fatalistic courage of the one who boasts, "Let us eat and drink for tomorrow we die," instead we follow King and look death and failure straight in the eye, crying boldly with the apostle, "Where, O death, is your victory? Where, O death, your sting?" (1 Cor. 15:55). For if the cross tells us that we are already dead, then the resurrection promises that we are also alive in Christ now and forever. And this is the second thing we learn from Paul. For while the cross frees us to live a life of abandon, the resurrection ensures that it is not the abandon of the desperate.

Oscar Cullmann captured just this sentiment in his work on the theology of Luke as he compared the life of the Christian to the situation of the Allied soldiers living and fighting between D-Day and VE Day.[11] Once the Allies had landed successfully on the beaches of Normandy, you see, their ultimate victory was ensured. There were, of course, months of fighting left, and during this time, soldiers would continue to give of their strength, their limbs, and their lives. But what a difference to give one's strength, limbs, and life in the cause of victory rather than defeat! So also, Conzelmann asserts, the Christian who lives between Christ's resurrection and Christ's return at the end of time lives a life of struggle, but it is a struggle infused by the hope and promise of God's eventual

---

11. Oscar Cullmann, *Christ and Time: The Primitive Christian Conception of Time and History*, trans. by Floyd V. Filson (Philadelphia: Westminster Press, 1964), 84.

triumph, living in anticipation of that day when God will come to wipe the tears away from every eye.

This is not easy. Make no mistake. For we find ourselves regularly and relentlessly caught between the already of what God has done in Christ's cross and resurrection and the not yet of what God has promised to do for us and all the world. We live, that is, in the meantime, in the "time being," and as W. H. Auden writes in his Christmas poem of that name, "the Time Being is, in a sense, the most trying time of all."[12]

That is why the hope born of Christ's resurrection is simply crucial. Baptized into Christ's death and resurrection, we can throw ourselves into the struggles of our day and time not expecting that our actions will save the world, but confident of God's promise to redeem the world, we are both able and eager to make a difference in the little corner of the world in which we find ourselves.

This is the transcendent hope that Camus laments he does not have but that is found in the biblical witness in spades. It is perhaps summed up most succinctly in the consistent message of the angels to those mortals they attend, whether Mary at the beginning of the Luke's Gospel or the women gathered by the empty tomb at the end. It is a message as brief as it is timely: *Do not be afraid.*

In this world ravaged by violence and inequity, we Christians are called to proclaim, "Do not be afraid." In this world marked in the sixty-five years between Camus's time and our own by wars both hot and cold, we are called to proclaim, "Do not be afraid." In this post-9/11, Code Orange world where even the dominant version of Christianity is based on fear (the fear of punishment and damnation), we are called to offer an alternative vision and proclaim, "Do not be afraid." For we are those persons who, accompanied by the one who has died and been raised again, will not be governed by fear and despair but by faith, courage, mercy, love—and a hope rooted in God's activity to raise Jesus from the dead.

A Story So Good It Must Be True

But if this proclamation is relevant, is it also credible? In some ways, the history of Christianity during modernity is the narrative of a losing battle against the charge that the Christian faith, finally, is *just* a story, one different perhaps in details but no different in character from any number of other grand stories, religious and nonreligious alike. For most of this time, Christians have objected

---

12. W. H. Auden, *For the Time Being: A Christmas Oratorio* (Princeton, NJ: Princeton University Press, 2013).

to characterizing our faith as a story and have gone to extreme measures to prove the validity of Christian claims at the secular bar of human reason set by the Enlightenment. Hence titles like *The Case for Christ* and *Evidence That Demands a Verdict* sought to demonstrate the rational, objective character of the Christian faith.

But I have become convinced that if we are to discover a way forward in a secular age devoid of meaningful stories, it may be that we are called to stop denying that charge but actually to embrace it: yes, Christianity is a story, we are willing to say, but oh, what a story!

While it may sound like a concession to admit that Christianity may finally be only a story, I don't mean it that way. Rather, and as we explored in the first chapter, whether we name it this way or not, we now swim in postmodern currents and so have come to recognize that what we used to call "Reality" is itself a story. It is a comprehensive story for sure, but still a story. Because whether you call it a grand narrative or a metanarrative or our standard story, we still have to admit that we—each and all of us—live our lives according to a set of assumptions about humanity, the world, and God that are grounded in narratives as unprovable as they are distinct.

During the modern era, we enjoyed a naïveté born of relative cultural isolation that led us to call our story "reality." That is no longer our situation. Living now in a world with two hundred channels on cable television, living in a world where it is as easy to read Al Jazeera as it is the *New York Times* on the Web, living in a world where our children know more about the world's religions than we do because they have classmates who are practitioners of those religions—living in this world, we are confronted by the fact that there are multiple stories out there, all of which purport to describe accurately the world we live in and none of which can be sustained or proven beyond all others.

This is what Jean-François Lyotard meant, as we discussed earlier, when he proclaimed the death of the metanarrative: that there is no longer any *single* story of reality that can hold the field uncontested. Rather, we live in the age of the competition of the metanarratives, where each and every day, any number of stories seek to make sense of our lives and experience and in this way gain our allegiance. While the chapters on pluralism will have more to say about this, for now it is important to note that these stories are not simply, or even primarily, religious, but rather are also political, nationalistic, and cultural. In fact, I'd wager that the greatest threat to the Christian story in this land is not a Jewish, Buddhist, or Islamic story, but rather the Western consumer-consumption story that denies any transcendent reality and therefore establishes worth on the basis of material possessiones. Such a materialist worldview, undergirded by no sense of transcendent worth, all too quickly comes to view our children as nothing more than potential consumers waiting to be exploited as players in a game far less bloody but no less damaging than Collins's Hunger Games.

There are times, of course, when we are called to denounce these other stories as false gospels that promise fulfillment and contentment but provide only disappointment. But more often, I think, the task is less to denounce them and more to ask our people whether these stories are sufficient to bear the weight of meaning that we need from them. That is, is the story about accumulation and consumption adequate to give us the meaning and hope, the sense of community and acceptance, we crave? The minute we do so, we recognize the dead-end into which the secular world has led us: none of the material stories offered in place of a transcendent one has been sufficient to stir our hearts and imaginations. As Taylor writes, "People sense a terrible flatness in the everyday, and this experience has been identified particularly with the commercial, industrial, or consumer society. They feel emptiness of the repeated, accelerating cycle of desire and fulfillment in consumer culture; the cardboard quality of bright supermarkets, or neat row housing in a clean suburb."[13]

Here is where it becomes crucial for us to recognize Christianity as a story, an *alternative* story about a transcendent reality that also seeks to make sense of our immediate and material lives and experience. Preaching and worship, from this point of view, take on tremendous significance as the primary place where we tell that story and offer it to our people as something they can entertain, enact, and live into. In this sense, we are charged with telling and repeating the ancient story again and anew, that its transcendent claims might become seriously imaginable for those who gather in the assembly and lead their lives in the secular world.

To do this effectively, however, we must first recognize that the transcendent story we tell is—there's just no other way to say it—highly improbable. In fact, one might be tempted to call it fantasy. But before getting too upset with this particular choice of words, please note that I didn't suggest that it's untrue, but rather that it's fantasy, as in fantastical, beyond our experience, extraordinary, not of this world. And I would argue that precisely because it is *not* of this world, precisely because it *is* beyond our physical and material existence and experience, it has the power to redeem us.

To put things most baldly, I believe the Christian story as witnessed to in Scripture and enacted in our preaching and worship *not* because it tells me

---

13. Taylor, *A Secular Age*, 309.

things I've seen and know for myself, but precisely because it describes a reality that stretches beyond the confines of my finite, mortal existence and therefore has the capacity to redeem me, and you, and this life and world we share. If all we can see, in other words, is ultimately all there is, then we frankly have no chance.

So while we may have evidence for this transcendent reality, we have no proof. We may have tasted the reality of God's life, but we can only point to it, not capture and prove it. This is, perhaps, part of what Paul and later the Reformers meant when they declared that we live "by faith alone."

In fact, I think the church has failed to address the secular age with a compelling narrative in large part because it has accepted the terms of the demystified world secularism boasts, always reducing the claims of the church to ones accepted by a world that has abandoned transcendence. The gospel was reduced to those things we can see, assess, and measure, whether personal fulfillment, a stand against societal ills, or pragmatic and personal application of timeless moral truth. Of course, all of these things can be valid elements of the Christian life, but robbed of their place in a larger transcendent story about God's intention and quest to redeem humanity from death, each ends up a tragic reduction of what centuries of Christians have lived and died for.

Perhaps not surprisingly, to sketch the heart of the Christian narrative and promise in appropriately grand terms, we often must look beyond our prose descriptions to the venue of poetry and song to describe it aptly. Near the beginning of *For the Time Being*, W. H. Auden, for instance, has the shepherds marching toward Bethlehem make the following confession: "We who are about to die demand a miracle . . . . [for] Nothing can save us that is possible."[14]

And there it is. When you are on the brink of death (from illness or failure or disappointment or heartbreak or calamity or oppression or depression or whatever), you are keenly aware that you are insufficient, that this world, this reality is temporary. You realize that you stand in desperate need of the miraculous, of salvation, because that which is merely possible cannot save.

And this is what the gospel offers, what Karl Barth described as the "impossible possibility"—a reality that transcends the everyday real, a Truth deeper than all else we have been told is true, a story that stretches beyond and encompasses all our stories so as to give them meaning, integrity, and purpose.

Now some, I know, convinced of the secular dismissal of the transcendent, would call this an escape, a flight from reality and the specter of death. And indeed, this is the great risk, the significant gamble of the Christian life. For

---

14. Auden, *For the Time Being: A Christmas Oratorio* (Princeton, NJ: Princeton University Press, 2013)

the truth the gospel proclaims is not some mere datum or fact we can verify, but rather is a claim, a confession, even a wager that there is a Reality and Truth beyond the confines of our mortal, meager existence that we will not fully experience until the world as we know it passes away, and then and only then will we see through the glass clearly and understand fully, even as we are fully understood.

But make no mistake, it *is* a risk, one that we cannot calculate or estimate ahead of time but that we throw ourselves into, mind, body, and spirit, simply because we cannot help it—because, that is, we have been taken captive to the word of God through our encounter with Scripture, drawn into this world of faith the way Lucy was drawn through the wardrobe into Narnia and, having tasted the transcendent promises of God, cannot return. So there it is: the gospel is true, *and* it is fantastic, otherworldly, beyond our experience.

At the same time, however, the Christian tradition confesses that this fantastic, transcendent story intersects with our own immanent one. In a marvelous essay entitled "A Vote of Thanks to Cyrus," Dorothy Sayers describes realizing as a young girl that the Cyrus of her history classes was the same as that of the Bible. The rush of adrenaline that intersection gave her came from realizing that the biblical writers were simultaneously telling a fantastic story *and* claiming that it collided with her own—indeed, that the biblical story *was* her own story.[15] So let me say it again: the gospel is true, *and* it is fantastic, otherworldly; it is beyond our experience and played out in our experience.

At times, however, after years of tailoring our message to a world devoid of transcendence, I wonder if we've forgotten just how audacious, even ridiculous the gospel is—how contrary it is to all our reason and experience, even as it claims to be rooted in our history. No wonder Paul calls the gospel story foolishness, for it isn't simply good news, but rather news that is *too* good to be true. Consider: week in and week out, we preach and listen to a gospel story that asserts not only that there is a God who has created and still sustains the vast cosmos, but that this God not only knows that you exist, but gives a damn, actually cares, deeply and passionately about us and our ups and downs, hopes and fears, successes and failures, cares enough to send God's only Son into the world to die that we might have life.

What else is that message if it is not, quite literally, *in-credible*—that is, not believable? Because in the face of the evening news, this news is simply too good to be true.

---

15. Sayers's "A Vote of Thanks to Cyrus" can be found in print in *Letters to a Diminished Church: A Passionate Argument for the Relevance of Christian Doctrine* (Nashville: Thomas Nelson, 2004).

Or maybe it's so good that it has to be true. That was the opinion of J. R. R. Tolkien, author of *The Lord of the Rings* and an Oxford professor. Tolkien, a devout Roman Catholic, argued in an essay written half a century ago that the gospel story is not only the perfect fairy tale but also actually the root of all fantasy because it tells the deeply true and ultimately joyful story of humanity, fallen and redeemed, in all of its horror, poignancy, and glory.[16]

Imagine that, for a moment: that Lewis's Narnia and Tolkien's Middle-earth, Rowling's Hogwarts, Lucas's Star Wars, and even Collins's Panem are all—some directly, others less so; some intentionally, others by accident—only reflections of the deeply true and ultimately joyful story of wayward humanity and God's passionate, tenacious quest to redeem us through love.

Our task in Christian preaching when confronted with a secular society is therefore not to accede to demands for a demystified story but rather to call the terms of this secular world into question. Our task, that is, is to listen for the deep yearning in our people for a story that is worthy of their devotion and therefore to tell—and by telling make real and imaginable once again—the improbable, even fantastic Christian story and thereby invite our hearers into biblical faith. Faith understood this way, of course, is less like certain knowledge and more like an invitation to an adventure, an adventure described throughout the pages of Scripture and which, at almost any single point, is simultaneously too good to be true and so good it must be true.

Here again, the apostle Paul serves us well. Pressed to defend his own ministry in Corinth, Paul invited his hearers away from their conception that authority is rooted in the rhetorical prowess or logical acumen of the speaker and toward considering the possibility that authority comes from the subject matter to which the speaker is a servant. As he writes, "Think of us in this way, as servants of Christ and stewards of the mysteries of God" (1 Cor. 4:1). Paul, that is, lodges both his authority and responsibility in the story of Jesus, the climax in the mysterious and unfolding story of God's love for the creation. It is a story that at every turn is as incredible as it is unpredictable.

From Genesis's claim that God created the whole earth and placed humanity at the center of it all to care for it and each other to Revelation's promise that in time God will come to wipe every tear from our eyes and create a new heaven and earth, the Bible is full to bursting with one unbelievable promise after another. At the heart of it all stands the audacious, foolish, even unthinkable confession that in Jesus—born, Sayers would remind us, while

---

16. See Tolkien's essay "On Fairy Stories," in *Essay Presented to Charles Williams*, ed. C. S. Lewis (London: Oxford University Press, 1947), 38–89.

Augustus was emperor and Quirinius was governor (Luke 2:1-2)—God almighty took on our lot and our life, dying the death of an outcast, so that we might have life and have it abundantly in this world and the next.

The really amazing thing about this story, of course, is that it not only tells us about the people of faith who have gone before us, but actually invites us into that same fantastic story that is always lived out in the intersection of the ordinary and extraordinary, the transcendent and the immanent, the sacred and the secular. The Bible, after all, begins at the very beginning in Genesis and doesn't end until the very end in Revelation, which means that you and I and the people we preach to live right now somewhere between the Acts of the Apostles and Revelation. Each time we preach, therefore, we are calling our people to take up their part in this story, to struggle to believe in a world of doubt, to love in a world of hate, to make peace in a world of violence, and to offer hope in a world of despair.

We do so not with the hopeless courage of Camus, but rather with the hopeful promise of the apostle Paul that whether we succeed or fail, we may still take heart, for the God who created the world out of nothing and raised Jesus Christ from the dead will not give up on us, has not given up on us, and will work through our ordinary words for the health and redemption of this world.

Our call, from this point of view, is to tell this sacred story, to announce the impossible possibility, to offer our people a transcendent hope right here, in the meantime of their ordinary, historically bounded, and all-too-often flat lives. It is not the only option before us, of course. Some have and will continue to assert with dogmatic certainty that the truth of Christianity can be proven like any other rational fact, while others will continue to couch their proclamation in the tentative terms demanded by a world suspicious of stories and devoid of mystery and transcendence. So the choice to preach with audacity and courage a story that cannot be proven but only proclaimed, entertained, and lived is always before you.

But then again, maybe it's not really a choice. Maybe for those, like us, who have been called, all we can do is answer, knowing that the way forward is neither clear nor easy, but that we are compelled nevertheless to continue the journey. Hope, after all, is indeed a dangerous thing and leads us often to dare great deeds we would not otherwise have attempted. So perhaps for those of us who have been taken captive by the hope of Christ, there is no question, no choice, no decision at hand, but only obedience to a summons.

4

Preaching the Grandeur of God in the Everyday

Given that in the previous chapter I named the dominant challenge of the secular age as a "crisis of immanence" that has resulted in a loss of hope, it may seem obvious that our challenge and call is to proclaim the transcendent promises of God in order to create and sustain vibrant Christian hope. And indeed, as I suggested, that is part of the challenge—but only part.

We live in a secular world and preach to a secular people. Here I mean "secular" in its most original form: *saecularis,* Latin for "being of the world." That is, for the last several centuries, we have been trained and taught to seek answers to our questions about the natural order, universe, and society through our study of the creation (science), not via reflection on the Creator (theology). Explanation, not story, is the watchword of the age of reason. In short, we live, as Auden describes it in *For the Time Being,*

> . . . in the moderate Aristotelian city
>> Of darning and the Eight-Fifteen, where Euclid's geometry
>> And Newton's mechanics would account for our experience,
>> And the kitchen table exists because I scrub it.[1]

I say this with no regret or reproach. Give up medicine, technology, scientific progress, electricity, and more? Not on your life. So we are Christians, but we are secular Christians. This means, among other things, that we simply cannot go back to a version of Christianity that assumes a three-tiered universe filled with angels and demons and where God's activity is obvious and omnipresent. That version of the Christian narrative (and it is helpful to keep in mind that it is only one version) has been on the wane since at least the Enlightenment,

---

1. W. H. Auden, *For the Time Being: A Christmas Oratorio* (Princeton, NJ: Princeton University Press, 2013).

and simply trying to reinstate it will not work, at least not in most of our congregations.[2]

We need, then, to explore more precisely the nature of the crisis of hope we named in the previous chapter if we are to address it directly. So let me put it this way: secularism has resulted in a loss of hope not simply or even primarily in an eternal future, but rather in the value and meaningfulness of the present. Our people, that is, are not asking Luther's question of whether they will find a merciful God in the afterlife, but rather whether what we spend our time and energy on in *this* life has even a modicum of enduring worth or value.

Hence, more and more people search not just for hope in general but also for a sense of purpose, of meaning, and of coherency: Does the life we are constructing and living make sense? Many people, if they are willing to come clean, will confess to having experienced at some point in their lives the sense, as Walter Taylor describes, that "what previously satisfied us, gave us a sense of solidity, seems not really to match up, not to deserve what we put into it."[3] To put that in more overtly theological language, with a loss of transcendence has also come the loss of a sense of *telos*, a purposeful and meaningful goal toward which we strive.

Once again, I believe that the Christian narrative is remarkably well poised to address this situation, but only if we can reclaim a vibrant theology of vocation. This may not seem like a revolutionary suggestion. But in the preliminary stages of research regarding Christian vocation, a team of colleagues and I discovered two significant and contradictory dimensions about our contemporary situation. First, we discovered that the graduates of the five schools working together on this project—each school representing a different Christian tradition—highly value vocation and report their commitment to teach and preach it. Second, however, we also discovered that very few people from the congregations being served by our graduates actually "feel" called.[4] That is, they struggle to believe that what they do matters to God or the church. Up to this point, in other words, their faith has provided little help in discovering hope, meaning, and purpose in their daily lives.

---

2. In some ways, this has been the strategy of fundamentalism, to insist on a narrative and worldview at significant odds with that of the culture. But as the world grows ever smaller and such subcultures are harder to keep isolated, that more "isolationist" approach is crumbling.

3. Taylor, *A Secular Age* (Cambridge, MA: Belknap Press of Harvard University Press, 2007), 307.

4. As of this writing, "The Christians' Callings in the World" project, generously funded by the Lilly Endowment, is still in progress and involves research teams from the Catholic Theological University (Roman Catholic), Duke Divinity School (Methodist), Fuller Seminary (Evangelical), Luther Seminary (Lutheran), and Princeton Theological Seminary (Reformed).

My suggestion, then, is that in order to equip our people to overcome the "crisis of immanence" they are experiencing on this side of the secular age, we need to awaken them to the possibility that, as Gerard Manley Hopkins once wrote, "The world is charged with the grandeur of God."[5] God, we confess, is still active, not only in the beauty of the natural world but also in our broken but grace-filled relationships and roles as friend, partner, student, employer and employee, citizen, volunteer, and more. Moreover, I believe that the Sunday sermon is a principal place from which to lend our people the conviction that, seen from the perspective of baptismal faith, there is no small or meaningless gesture, and that what we sometimes think of as "mundane" or "ordinary" or even "secular" life is simply bursting with possibility for meaning and purpose.

We are at a place, in other words, where we can no longer afford to stress either the immanent or the transcendent alone. Left to its own devices, immanence always falls short, unable to validate itself or offer others meaning. At the same time, as Sallie McFague writes and as experience in the secular world has shown, "The more God's transcendence is stressed at the expense of God's immanence, the less relevant God becomes."[6] Hence we have an opportunity to teach and preach that it is precisely this immanent world that is charged, in Hopkins's words, with the grandeur of the transcendent God.

To get at that task, this chapter divides into three sections, the first sketching a bare-bones and broadly ecumenical theology of vocation, and the second suggesting several widespread practices that, while perhaps salutary on their own, have made it difficult for our people to hear, believe, and live into a theology of calling. While each of these may seem to take us rather far afield from the subject of preaching, they are critical to set the stage for a conversation in the third about how we can preach in a way that nurtures a robust "vocational imagination" that will equip our people with a sense of meaning and purpose that the secular world has failed to provide.

VOCATION IN A NUTSHELL

What became apparent very early in the research project I mentioned is the degree to which the representatives of these five distinct theological traditions held a largely shared understanding of how God calls God's people into meaningful service in the world. The heart of that understanding can be summarized in four points.

---

5. Hopkins, Gerard Manley, "God's Grandeur," in *Poems and Prose* (New York: Penguin, 1985). 27.

6. Sallie McFague, *Life Abundant* (Minneapolis: Fortress Press, 2000), 134.

1. God loves the world and seeks not only to redeem it at the end of time but also to care for and sustain it in the meantime. This "in the meantime" is often the overlooked work of God. But as the leaders of the Protestant Reformation regularly confessed, not only does God care for and tend our eternal lives and spiritual well-being through the proclamation of the gospel, God also cares for and tends our daily lives and temporal well-being through our families, communities, businesses, and government. It is, in other words, God's intention to bless the world through both sacred and secular institutions.

2. All people, Christian or not, are invited into this work of caring for and sustaining God's beloved world and people. Those who are baptized into Christian faith and identity are blessed to recognize their work as God-ordained and God-pleasing and to receive the counsel and encouragement of their faith communities as they seek to discern and respond to God's call. But even those who are not part of the Christian community, we confess, nevertheless play a part through their roles and service to make God's world a more trustworthy and healthful place.

3. Opportunities for partnering with God to care for the world are manifold. Indeed, wherever you may find yourself has the potential to be a "vocational arena." Work, family life, volunteering, school, civic engagement, community activities—all these and more present opportunities to serve God by serving your neighbor. Further, responding to God's call includes more than direct help, comfort, or assistance to those in need. It also includes making the world a more trustworthy place through all kinds of different labor and effort. The person working at a telecommunications office, for instance, may not only provide a listening ear to a colleague or volunteer at a charity, her work each day to maintain the communications system so many people depend upon also serves countless neighbors she may never meet.

4. God works through our Sunday gatherings and congregational life to remind us of our baptismal identity and strengthen us for Christian service. Worship, from this point of view, not only proclaims the gospel but also prepares Christians to enter into the world looking for opportunities to serve God in the ordinary and everyday aspects of their life. Congregational life is similarly outward focused, as we see congregations as places where Christians can receive the counsel of others, the teaching of the tradition, and the encouragement of the faith to serve God by serving neighbor and world in their daily lives.

While this four-part outline of a widely shared theology of vocation is relatively straightforward, its implications for the Christian life are profound. Seen from this point of view, *all* of our everyday activities have the potential to be seen as sacred work, and the ordinary places of our lives—the office, kitchen, or locker room—as holy ground in that they afford opportunities to join God in God's tireless work to love and bless this world. The immanent, as it turns out, far from being devoid of God's presence, is thoroughly imbued with the transcendent, and even the most mundane of activities, if done in good faith and with attention to the need of one's neighbor and world, can take on a holy significance.

THE SUNDAY-MONDAY DISCONNECT

With such a simple yet compelling theology of vocation at our disposal, the question quickly becomes why it has proven largely ineffectual. While the contributing factors are probably manifold, I want to focus on one: we have unintentionally affirmed the secular impulse to restrict God's activity and therefore have made it increasingly difficult for our people to imagine being "called" in their daily lives in the secular world. In particular, we have so greatly stressed the importance of Sunday activities that we have unintentionally devalued the lives we lead during the rest of the week.

By way of example, ask almost any of your people what the most important day of the week is in relation to faith, and they will most likely answer, "Sunday." This makes sense, as Sunday is the day Christians gather to hear the word, share the sacraments, and receive the consolation and encouragement of fellow believers. Gathering on Sunday for these purposes is, to borrow the old words, "meet, right, and salutary" as it honors the third commandment to "keep the Sabbath holy." Almost every Christian tradition therefore honors Sunday as, if no longer a day of rest in the strictest sense, at least a day in which to withdrawal from daily pursuits in order to hear the word.

All of this is well and good, except for one thing. We have unintentionally communicated to our people that Sunday is not only an important day, but also the *most* important day. It is sacred not only in the sense of being "set aside" for worship but also in the sense of being far above the rest of the week. Over time, this way of thinking tends to give the impression that the other days of the week (and what we do on them) are far less important. Moreover, we've tended to emphasize church activities as the places where we *really* meet and serve God, inadvertently suggesting that we are far less likely to do so in our ordinary lives of work, home, relationships, and the rest. We do not imply this intentionally, I realize, but we still nevertheless communicate with some frequency and power that Sunday matters a lot more than Monday.

I suspect that as you read these last few sentences, you had an urge to argue with the statement that we have emphasized Sunday activities to the point that our people have a truncated sense of the importance of the rest of the week and their daily lives. Let me therefore offer a simple illustration that you can try out in your own setting. At the outset of his book *God at Work*, David Miller shares an exercise he often does when speaking with groups of clergy or laypersons.

> When speaking to clergy gatherings of a variety of denominations around the country, I often ask this question: "Who here prays for and commissions your teenagers as they go off on a mission trip?" Invariable, all hands go up. "Who here prays for and commissions your Sunday School teachers in September as the new church year begins. Finally, I ask: "Who here prays for all certified public accountants around April 15, and who here prays for all the salespeople and those working on commission at the end of the month and end of the year, when quotas are due?" Silence. Eyes drop the ground. Usually not a single hand is raised.[7]

Miller has said that when he does this exercise with a group made up largely of clergy, there is usually an embarrassed chuckle when the point sinks in. But when he has done this exercise with groups of businesspersons, the reaction is more of a derisive laugh. Businesspeople simply do not expect recognition or support for their labors from their church leaders, except perhaps during the stewardship campaign.

Obviously, it's not that praying for our Sunday school teachers, key volunteers, or youth group is wrong. Rather, it's that when these and other folks volunteering at church are the only people we pray for, we give the distinct impression that what really matters is Sunday, church, and the things we do at church. Moreover, the lack of attention we give to the everyday activities, employment, and associations of our people sends a clear signal that those activities don't merit the attention of church and, by extension, God.

A picture from a conference on Christian vocation helps illustrate our current situation. The attendees, most of whom were lay people, were asked to consider together the challenges they experienced in connecting faith and life. But in addition to participating in small group conversations typical of these kinds of conferences, the participants were also invited to a draw a picture that portrayed their experience. Colored pencils, crayons, and paper in hand, the group went to work, first sketching individual drawings, then sharing them

---

7. David W. Miller, *God at Work: The History and Promise of the Faith at Work Movement* (New York: Oxford University Press, 2006), 10.

around the table, and eventually combining them into a single picture that captured their struggle. (I've included that picture below.)[8]

As you can see, they've drawn a chasm between their faith and their everyday lives. But what else do you notice? Two things stick out to me. First, the world they can touch is what they often refer to as "the real world." The world of school and work and home and the all the rest is concrete and palpable, while they strain to be in touch with the church. Second, the sun is shining over the church, but only clouds attend their daily lives. Why? I think it's because, per David Miller's exercise, they know God is happy when they're at church, but God's disposition to the rest of their lives is ambiguous at best.

All of this leads me to the ineluctable conclusion that while we've certainly obeyed the commandment to "observe the Sabbath," we've unintentionally done so in a way that has devalued everyday life. Little wonder that our people have great difficulty imagining that their lives as teachers, friends, parents, citizens, students, volunteers, and more are in any concrete sense "callings." They have not heard them named as such by those in religious authority. So if they despair of the possibility that their daily lives and activities hold any enduring and transcendent value, perhaps that's because they have learned, as

8. The drawing is a response to the work of Richard Broholm and John Hoffman, *Developing the Laity for Their Full Ministry* (Boston: The Center for the Ministry of the Laity, 1985).

much by what we've *not* said as by what we have, that the sure and certain location of God's activity is church and that a "calling" refers only to activities performed there.

PREACHING TO HELP US SEE GOD

On the morning of January 12, 2007, a team from the *Washington Post* conducted an experiment. They placed a video camera in one of the stations for the Metro, the mass transit system that serves Washington, DC, and the surrounding communities. The camera recorded the reactions of the people who passed by a street musician playing the violin on their way to catch the subway for work or school or wherever they might be going. Over the course of the forty-five minutes the musician played, a little more than one thousand people passed by the musician. And almost no one stopped to listen.

What makes the experiment interesting is that the violin player wasn't your ordinary street musician. It was Joshua Bell, one of the finest classical violinists in the world, and he was playing six of the most difficult and beautiful pieces of his repertoire on his $3.5 million Stradivarius violin. And almost no one stopped to listen. A week earlier, he'd played some of these same pieces to a sold-out crowd at a concert in Boston, where the cheap seats were a hundred bucks. Later, Bell reported that the acoustics of that subway station were nearly perfect. Yet although more than a thousand people passed by, almost nobody stopped to listen.

In his article capturing the experiment, Gene Weingarten, a staff writer for the *Washington Post*, suggests a series of interrelated and interesting questions: Have we become too busy to notice beauty? Further, have we, as a culture, trained ourselves even to *see* beauty if it's anywhere other than where we expect beauty to be? Would we value a painting, that is, if it were removed from a museum and hung in a restaurant? Can we even hear beautiful music if it's not surrounded by a concert hall? And what do our answers to these questions reveal about us?[9]

I think we could ask similar questions about the current state of our life in the church. Have our people become too busy accomplishing the immanent tasks of day-to-day life to notice a transcendent God made present in and through those tasks? Have we trained our people to detect God's presence when God isn't surrounded by stained glass and pipe organ music? Have we prepared them to encounter God—and to be used by God—in their everyday life? In

9. Gene Weingarten, "Pearls before Breakfast," *Washington Post*, April 8, 2007, http://www.washingtonpost.com/wp-dyn/content/article/2007/04/04/AR2007040401721.html.

short, have equipped our people to see God anywhere other than Sunday-morning worship? And if we haven't, what kind of future can we expect—or do we deserve?

Preaching alone, of course, cannot solve this problem. But it is an indispensable part of the solution. Nowhere else are we more likely to encounter our people and help shape their vision to detect God's presence in, among, and through the activities that make up their daily lives. To encourage preaching that strengthens their "vocational imagination," here are three suggestions.

1. Visit your people in their vocational arenas, and describe those visits in your preaching. I am skeptical about the word *transformation.* Whether because of my theological anthropology or personal experience, I tend to think that while people can certainly grow, I am uncertain we can essentially change. For this reason, I rarely use the word *transformation* to describe, well, almost anything. The consistent exception I make, however, is when describing the effect the simple practice of visiting parishioners outside the church has on preachers. And I make the exception because those pastors who commit to taking time each week to visit their parishioners at their various vocational venues often describe the impact of those visits on their sermons with a single word: transformational.

Their preaching, they often report, becomes more three-dimensional as they find it easier to address their insights about the gospel not to an imagined context but to the actual settings in which their people live out their lives of faith. Moreover, preachers report that their hearers notice the change as well. Congregation members talk about sermons being more "on target" and "connected to real life," among other things.

When I've brought up this idea in various continuing-education settings, there are always a few pastors—at least a few brave enough to speak up—who wonder whether their people actually *want* to be visited at their places of work or school. Their homes perhaps, as most people are used to that, but having a pastor show up at school, work, or a place of volunteering seems a little odd.

To be honest, I tend to think this concern is misplaced and probably reflects more of our own insecurity than it does our people's concerns. I sometimes wonder, actually, whether we have acceded to the secularist impulse that, stemming from a diminished sense of the transcendent, restricts faith to the private spheres of life. Perhaps it's *we* who feel odd or out of place in the public venues of our people's lives, at least when we come as a pastor.

But time and again when I've visited people in their various vocational venues, they've introduced me to their fellow students, employees, friends, and volunteers with a note of pride in their voices. And the pastors who have taken me up on this suggestion regularly share the same. For whether we realize it or not, our presence validates what people do as being worthy of the church's attention. Indeed, because we are a reminder of God's presence, when we arrive at someone's school or workplace, we convey that what the person does merits God's attention as well.

Three further thoughts stem from my own experience and interviews with pastors after they have made this practice a part of their ministry. First, you can announce your intention to make visits from the pulpit and in the newsletter and bulletin, but you may have to initiate some of the early visits. People, quite frankly, may not believe you at first. In fact, in a poll conducted a few years ago, respondents were asked to rank several persons in their lives—spouse, colleague, neighbor, doctor, pastor, etc.—in relation to whom they would be most likely to ask about a problem they were having at work. Pastors finished last, not because the respondents didn't think they were well intentioned, but rather because they didn't think they would know enough about the "real world" to be helpful. As you make more visits, however, word will get around, and people we will respond to your invitation and look forward to seeing you in their world.

Second, on the visit, allow some time for conversation. Ask your host to describe what he or she does in this vocational world, what the joys and challenges are, and how you and the congregation can be supportive of the distinct ministry your host carries on in this place. "Ministry" in this case doesn't mean simply sharing their faith (though you may hear stories about that) but rather captures the ways in which they partner with God to create and sustain a more trustworthy world. Also ask where they see God in this place. But be prepared to help with an answer, as we have not trained our people to look for God anywhere outside of church. Over time, however, speaking of "seeing God" and "partnering with God" and being God's "co-creators" will become part of the language of the congregation, and when that happens, you'll know you have nurtured a robust vocational imagination.

Third, mention these visits in your preaching. This may seem rather obvious, given our discussion thus far, but using these visits as examples in preaching reinforces to the congregation that you are serious about getting to know them, lifts up the manifold ways God is at work through their lives, and models the practice of putting their stories in the context of the biblical story. Imagine, for instance, how powerful it would be for one of your youth to hear you cite a visit to her school as a place where you learned how to think more deeply about the biblical passage in question, or what effect it might have on one of your parishioners to hear how you saw God at work in the dugout of the Little League team he coaches. Opportunities like this are as priceless as they are faithful to our theology and available to pastors willing to step outside the church building.

2. Preach to the middle zone of our lives. As part of a grant project studying vibrant preaching, I had the chance recently to read over the results of a survey taken by more than a thousand people who regularly listen to sermons and the in-depth interviews given by about two hundred more. The results have been fascinating, and to be honest, I'm still processing them. But so far, one thing already stands out that is perfectly in line with the subject we've been pursuing in this chapter: People *want* to understand why the biblical stories they hear read at church matter. Desperately. More than that, they want what happens on Sunday to matter throughout the week.

When I shared this observation with a group of preachers participating in a continuing-education event, one voiced the feelings of many in the group: "Aren't we doing that already?" My response was yes—and no. Yes, of course, we are working hard to open up these biblical passages, to help people understand them, and to offer people ways to think about their life in light of the faith. This generation of preachers is as talented, hardworking, and faithful in this respect as any other.

At the same time, I've become aware of an interesting trend in preaching that was confirmed by the survey results. It has to do with the focus or even locus of the sermon, something that came out regularly with regard to sermon illustrations. (And by "sermon illustrations," I'm not talking about canned stories but honest-to-goodness attempts to help us link the sermon's message to everyday life.)

Most of the illustrations I hear—and this was confirmed by many of the survey and interview respondents—are directed to what I would describe as one of two zones or spheres of our life in this world. The first is the *congregational zone.* That is, the sermon relates the biblical passage or theological theme to what's going on in the congregation's life, ministries, budget, outreach, volunteer opportunities, and the rest. The second sphere that a lot of sermon illustrations tend to explore is what I'd call the *global zone.* Here the preacher takes up the matter of wars, natural disasters, global challenges like malaria or hunger, or systemic problems, and in the sermon invites us to view these things from the standpoint of faith.

At this point, I want to be most clear: both of these zones are incredibly important to preach to. God is at work in and through the life of the congregation and cares deeply about—and wants us to care deeply about—the whole world. But as important as these two are, what often seems to be missing are all those things that constitute our lives in between our congregational involvement and the world's very real problems. As it turns out, this is *most of our lives*. Jobs, looking for a job, relationships, parenting, managing too many things at once, money, family, school, hobbies, volunteering, the media, local current events—that is, the stuff that constitutes our daily lives—often seems to be painfully absent from much of our preaching.

Again, let me be clear: I'm *not* advocating for a simplistic application of the sermon to one of life's problems, as if the answer to our people's hunger for a sense of the transcendent in their daily lives is to offer a series of sermons on stress management or the secrets of a better marriage. Such "application" preaching risks trivializing the sermon and rendering the gospel into merely good advice. At the same time, I *would* like to hear more preachers try to help us see how these ancient stories offer us a lens, a perspective that helps us make sense of some of the ordinary and mundane things that make up most of our life.

Karl Barth and Dietrich Bonhoeffer used to scoff at talk of "relevant preaching," where the Bible is instrumentalized into a self-help book. At the same time, they both—and Bonhoeffer especially—invited preachers to imagine that their job wasn't so much to interpret Scripture as it was to open up a passage such that it could interpret our daily lives.[10] This focus on how faith affects the mundane and ordinary elements of our lives—that is, the *majority* of our lives—is what I'd call "the middle zone" of preaching, and I would love to hear the sermon focus on it more often. And as it turns out, so would a majority of the people we surveyed and interviewed.

3. Allow others to testify to where they see God at work in and through their lives. Over time, as people become more confident of their ability to see God in the various dimensions of their lives and to connect the biblical story and their own story, they will be ready to share those observations in worship. Whether one or more members offer a sermon by sharing their experiences of looking for and discovering God in their daily lives, or whether you interview persons on how a particular passage shapes the way they look at the opportunities and challenges they are facing, the experience is powerful.

It is powerful for the ones participating because it is a tremendous affirmation of the worth and importance of their daily lives. It is a powerful experience for the congregation because they get to see "someone just like them" speak publicly about their faith. It's one thing, after all, to hear the

---

10. See Dietrich Bonhoeffer, *Worldly Preaching: Lectures on Homiletics*, ed. and trans. with critical commentary by Clyde E. Fant, rev. ed. (New York: Thomas Nelson, 1991), esp. pp. 111–16.

professional Christian (a.k.a. the preacher) talk about faith, quite another to see persons as "untrained" as they are make connections between their faith lives and daily lives. Over time, it may even give the rest of the congregation a sense that if these folks can do this, perhaps they can, too.

It is also powerful for the preacher as you grow in your knowledge of and respect for the many ways in which your people are bearing witness to their faith in God and as you begin to share responsibility for proclamation with the congregation. Over time, through this and other practices your congregation may grow from being a place *where the word is preached* more fully into a *community of the word* where all the members take some responsibility for sharing the news of God's ongoing work to love, bless, and save the world.

My goal across these various suggestions is to reverse what I would describe as the "directional energy" of the congregation. Because we believe God is located most surely in the worship of the congregation on Sunday, we tend in our congregational life to experience the centripetal force of being drawn to the church as the center of our faith lives. That is all well and good, except when that is the only force we feel, leaving church on Sunday not particularly attuned to God's work in the world. But if we can imagine that the purpose of Sunday is not simply to have an encounter with God, but rather to have the encounter clarify our vision and increase our ability to see God in all the dimensions of our lives, then we may also experience the centrifugal force of being propelled from worship on Sunday to lives of meaning, purpose, and faith in the world throughout the week.

This ebb and flow—being drawn to worship to hear the gospel proclaimed and being sent from worship to live in light of that gospel in the world—is what I've sometimes called the respiratory system of the body of Christ. Breathed in to hear the promise of forgiveness; breathed out to live as forgiven people. Breathed in to be comforted and encouraged in our struggles; breathed out to continue struggling to make our households, communities, and world more trustworthy places. Breathed in to to be confirmed in our identity as God's beloved children; breathed out to care for God's beloved world in any number of the vocational venues in which we find ourselves. And on it goes.

Preaching designed to equip people not merely to survive but to flourish amid the crisis of immanence of the secular world begins with the bold confession we articulated in the previous chapter that the God who created the world out of nothing and raised Jesus from the dead is still alive and active in our world. But it also moves on to make a similarly bold confession that this same

God both deigns and desires to enter into the mundane and ordinary elements of our lives in order to use us to care for and bless the world God loves so much. Such preaching, that is, orients us to God's work in the meantime, in and through the regular opportunities and activities that consume our daily lives. It's not, after all, that the focus of the secular world on the material elements of our lives is misplaced, but rather only that the material is insufficient on its own to bear the weight of meaning we crave. Thus, we orient our people to God's presence in, with, and under our daily activities so that they, in turn, are hallowed by the purposes to which God will put them.

Even the most robust and regular vocational preaching can't do everything. Patterns of pastoral visitation, adult education, and congregational governance all matter as well. But giving attention in your sermon to God at work in and through our everyday lives can and will send a signal that the transcendent God who took on our flesh in the incarnation of Jesus continues to take on flesh in the daily opportunities, struggles, challenges, and joys of our life in the world. And as we realize that, suddenly we discover in the ordinary, immanent, and even mundane elements of our lives the promise of God's presence and purpose. We discover, that is, that the world—our secular, moderate, Aristotelian world of catching trains and scrubbing tables and hoping beyond hope for something more—is indeed "charged with the grandeur of God."

PART III

Pluralism

5

Ministry and Preaching in the Age of Digital Pluralism

Each of us, I suspect, has a story about a conversation with someone who used to go to church but no longer does. Actually, each of us probably has any number of stories told by folks we met at a party or struck up a conversation with while waiting at the doctor's office. These stories usually tumble out when we've disclosed what we do for a living, as if the person with whom we are in conversation feels simultaneously a pang of guilt about being absent from church and a desire to make it clear it's nothing personal. And in addition to the stories told us by embarrassed but candid strangers, I'd wager that you have heard something of the same from members of your extended or immediate family. Yes, each of us has this kind of story.

One of the most powerful that I've heard came from a friend of mine who, on a transatlantic flight, struck up a conversation about church with the man sitting next to him. As it turned out, this gentleman and his family had recently had a long conversation about whether to continue attending their local congregation. As he explained to my friend, the previous year they had become critically overextended. Between work, social commitments, and the activities of their two children—one in elementary school, one in junior high—they were exhausted by Christmas and struggled to make it to the end of the school year.

Determined that the coming year would be different, they had held a "family council" over lunch a few weeks earlier to review all of their commitments in light of how each helped them be the kind of individuals and family they wanted to be. After an hour and a half of conversation, they came to their decisions. And church was one of the things they had decided to *stop* doing. Girl Scouts remained, but church was out. "It's just not that meaningful," the man explained. "We go each week and finally realized we're not getting anything out of it. It's hard to believe I'm saying this," he continued. "Our parents took us, and once we had kids, we took them, too. But it just doesn't connect with the rest of our lives. So we're done."

This story—all too familiar to those who lead congregations—can easily be taken as one more sign of the decay of the mainline church in a secular society. I want to suggest, however, that something else is afoot beyond, or at least in addition to, secularism to which we should attend. For me, this story offers insight into some of the seismic shifts taking place in our cultural and societal views not just about church, but also about our lives in this world that, while connected loosely to secularism, might be more aptly defined as pluralism.

As I indicated in the introduction to this book, the distinctions among pluralism, secularism, and for that matter, postmodernism are multifaceted and subtle, and it would be foolish to try to draw too sharp a line between them. That becomes immediately clear as we take up the relationship between pluralism and secularism. For while we described secularism as being marked by the retreat of transcendence, we see in our pluralistic world a plethora of transcendent options available to us. How can this be? That is, how can we talk simultaneously of both the loss of the transcendent and its proliferation? Two explanations help make sense of this curiosity.

First, secularism did not, in fact, triumph as the reigning cultural mindset. Instead, religion—or at least spirituality—rebounded, and a yearning for the transcendent returned. As Harvey Cox, who heralded the rise of "the secular city" in 1965, more recently writes, however, it is not the outward-looking transcendence of a pre-secular religiosity. Rather, the distinction between the immanent and transcendent has blurred: "Scholars of religion refer to the current metamorphosis in religiousness with phrases like the 'move to horizontal transcendence' or the 'turn to the immanent.' But it would be more accurate to think of it as the rediscovery of the sacred in the immanent, the spiritual within the secular."[1]

Secularism, in short, despite its attempts to confine mystery and the divine to the private spheres of live, nevertheless failed to displace deep spiritual yearning. But while it may not have succeeded as a cultural movement, it nevertheless left its mark, if not eliminating religion, then at least relativizing it. Traditional religion no longer holds a corner on the spiritual market. Indeed, many who grew up in the secular milieu are simultaneously suspicious of "organized" religion and open to spirituality in a variety of forms and on their own terms.

1. Harvey Cox, *The Future of Faith* (San Francisco: HarperOne, 2009), 2.

This leads to the second explanation of how the contrasting impulses of secularism and pluralism are also strangely complementary. For while secularism's adamant rejection of the transcendent has receded, the renaissance of religious interest that has grown in recent years is not, finally, limited to formal religion or even to "spirituality" but has been expanded to include multiple and varied meaning-making systems. For this reason, the pluralism we describe and encounter in this chapter and the next includes religious faith but also moves beyond it, just as the options for making meaning available to our people include the traditional faith with which many of them grew up but run far beyond congregational life.

Understood in light of the pluralism that shapes our twenty-first-century world, the story my friend told me of one family's decision to "quit" church provides clues to some of the challenges facing those of us who care about congregational vitality in a pluralistic, post-religious world. For while the statistics about mainline decline (in attendance, membership, and giving) are as familiar as they are depressing, I suspect that few of us understand the deeper societal causes of this decline. For this reason, in this chapter, I will suggest that many of our present struggles in the church can be traced to a lack of recognition of some significant social changes regarding how we make meaning and construct identity in a world simply saturated by stories.

NARRATIVE IDENTITY

As we've noted at several points in our survey of the cultural zeitgeist, Jean-François Lyotard, the French postmodern theorist, declared some years ago that we live in the age of the death of the metanarrative.[2] A metanarrative, most simply, is a story so large that it explains all other stories. Most frequently, we don't think of metanarratives as stories at all but rather as "reality." It is only when we encounter another metanarrative—another grand story that explains everything—that we recognize the boundaries of our own narrative version of reality. Lyotard therefore says that having believed, and been disappointed by, our grand narratives, and recognizing a host of others, we live only with micro- or local narratives, stories we may believe but that we know are true and relevant only for those communities that hold them.

While some have used Lyotard's diagnosis to explain the loss of influence of the Christian narrative in a postmodern world (that is, it is one of those

2. Lyotard, Jean-François, *The Postmodern Condition: A Report on Knowledge*, trans. Geoff Bennington and Brian Massumi, Theory and History of Literature 10 (Minneapolis: University of Minnesota Press, 1984), 37–41.

grand narratives that no longs holds sway in the cultural imagination), I am not confident that we can live long without some grand narrative. Indeed, and as we saw in our discussion of postmodernism, it's remarkably difficult to avoid offering grand narratives and making truth claims. For this reason, and as I've suggested earlier, I think we live not in an era that has seen the end of metanarratives, but rather during an age that is simply saturated by grand stories, none of which, as Lyotard suggests, reigns self-evidently supreme.

Put most simply, we are surrounded by competing truth claims. Some of these are religious, but many more are about material wealth, nationalism, or ethnicity. Significantly, each and every truth claim, whether it be proclaimed from a pulpit, touted on the cover or a major magazine, or hidden in the logo of an expensive brand, is part of a larger story about what constitutes the good, the beautiful, and the true. And this is where our discussion of pluralism overlaps our earlier conversations about postmodernism. But whereas postmodernism perceives in this swirl of competing truth claims a deterrent to our ability to make them in the first place, pluralism seems blissfully ignorant of such limitations and instead happily embraces any and all grand narratives and storied realities.

In this context, the Christian story has not so much disappeared as it has shrunk. The proliferation of different and competing stories about reality, that is, has occupied more and more of our congregants' attention, crowding out the biblical story as *the* narrative by which to make sense of all others and rendering it just one among a multitude. As a consequence, the Christian story no longer enjoys the privileged place it once did in the larger culture and in the marketplace of ideas.

I say this neither to render judgment on the culture nor to pine nostalgically for bygone days, but rather simply to acknowledge our current situation. In a land of many faiths and belief systems, most of the cultural reinforcements that the church once depended on to lift up and teach its story have withered.

As a consequence, our people do not know the biblical story anymore, and this is problematic if not downright disastrous for one crucial reason: we make sense of pretty much everything in the context of a larger story. Take the following quotation, for instance: "You ask, what is our policy? I can say: It is to wage war, by sea, land and air, with all our might and with all the strength that God can give us!" Taken out of context, it sounds like a terribly belligerent threat that we might attribute to some terrorist group. Placed in its narrative context—Winston Churchill's first address to the British Parliament as the newly appointed prime minister in 1940—it becomes a stirring call to resistance against tyranny.

So also with biblical quotations, scenes, and stories. Apart from their larger narrative context, even stories as well known as the Prodigal Son and the Good Samaritan become hardly more than quaint morality tales, retaining the power, perhaps, to serve as a well-worn ethical example along the lines of Aesop's Fables, but hardly able to transform lives or invite a new and redemptive relationship with God. Similarly, key words and concepts of the Christian faith—justification, vocation, proclamation, and gospel, just to name a few—have little or no meaning because there is no larger pattern of reference in which to understand them.

Let me be clear: the challenge I name is not primarily the need to bolster biblical illiteracy, as if knowledge of biblical quotations, places, and names were the issue. Rather, we need to develop in our congregations a meaningful familiarity with the biblical story such that it can inform, shape, and assist our daily living. We struggle, that is, not simply with a lack of biblical knowledge but rather with an impoverished biblical imagination.

In a class I teach on Scripture and congregational life, for example, I have my students interview two persons from their home congregation and ask them a variety of questions about how they connect their faith with their daily life. One of those questions is, "What biblical stories provide you with comfort or courage when you are struggling with a problem at home or work?" I would guess that more than two hundred persons have been asked this question over the years I have taught this course, yet only one student has ever reported an interviewee being able to answer that question easily. Only one of two hundred church-attending persons interviewed, that is, could readily identify a biblical story with which to make sense of a challenge in everyday life. Similarly, Joy Moore of Fuller Theological Seminary reports that not even one of the two dozen lifelong churchgoers she interviewed—persons who, by the way, had been listening to sermons for an average of thirty years or more—could offer a coherent summary of the biblical plot.[3]

When you recognize how little influence the biblical story has in the everyday lives of our people, you gain some sense of the enormous challenge before us to nurture genuine Christian identity. We are, as many have pointed out, narrative beings—that is, we make sense of our lives in and through stories.[4] Further, we construct our identity through narrative; identity, after all, is little more than the story we tell ourselves about ourselves.[5] But given

3. Joy J. Moore, "Narrating a Canonical Witness: A Homiletic for the 21st Century" (Ph.D. diss., Brunel University, 2007).

the minor role the Bible evidently plays in the lives of most churchgoers, it becomes much easier to see why participation in a local congregation has failed so many persons in supplying a meaningful religious identity. Like the man whose family would continue participating in Girl Scouts but not church, more and more members of our congregations have lost any incentive to continue attending a church that doesn't meaningfully contribute to their understanding of, and life in, the world.

DIGITAL PLURALISM

In light of this predicament, a slew of questions often present themselves as imperative to answer: What happened? Did we suddenly stop teaching the Bible? Did something in our preaching and worship change? Did we become so liberal (or conservative) that our people no longer felt comfortable? Is there some curriculum or mission strategy that can reverse this trend?

While I am sympathetic to the desire to understand and address the reasons for our decline, I am also struck by the fact that these are all "internal" questions about what we are doing in the church. I'd like, instead, to pose an "external" question: What has happened in the world that has made it so difficult for our people to imagine the biblical story as a viable resource by which to make sense of their lives?

My response to this question is that we have entered an age where we make meaning and construct identity differently than in generations past because of the vast number of stories, worldviews, and meaning-making systems available to us via digital means. The radical change in information technology—and particularly the rise of the Internet and the unparalleled access it grants to a dizzying array of comprehensive narratives—explains in large part why former patterns of communication and community building are increasingly ineffective.

I have chosen to name the era prompting these changes "digital pluralism" both to recognize the significant diversity of meaning-making systems available to us and to acknowledge that we have access to most of them because of the digital world in which we live. Hence, while we usually use the term *pluralism* to describe the greater ethnic and cultural diversity that characterizes our world

4. Though there are many monographs on this, the seminal article that prompted many toward a "narrative turn" is Steven Crites, "The Narrative Quality of Existence," *Journal of the American Academy of Religion* 39 (1971): 291–311.

5. For a bracing view of the degree to which story affects not just our stated identity but patterns of action, and particularly consumption behaviors, see Seth Godin's *All Marketers Are Liars*, rev. ed. (New York: Portfolio, 2009).

today, I want to highlight the pluralism of ideas, values, and convictions that are mediated to us not only through face-to-face encounters with persons who are different from us but also via digital means like the Internet, digital television, satellite radio, and more.

To fill out what I mean by the concept of digital pluralism, I will first offer two brief definitions that illumine complementary aspects of this era and then illustrate the concept further by looking at several significant cultural shifts that have resulted from it. Both definitions express what I mean by digital pluralism:

> 1. Digital pluralism describes a world in which there are multiple and competing realities, stories, convictions, perspectives, and worldviews, most of which are mediated by digital means.
> 2. Digital pluralism describes the exponential proliferation of the means by which to distribute and access information to the point of super-saturation.

Both of these definitions are important. First, because of digital means by which to share information, we not only have available to us but also are regularly subjected to a vast array of competing narratives about reality. At the same time, the amount of information that comes at us grossly exceeds what we can possibly process, creating an overload or super-saturation of information of nearly unimaginable proportions. In fact, the "digital universe" (all the bits of information captured and transmitted digitally) is expected to increase ten times every five years To put that figure into perspective, the amount of digital information created in 2008 was 487 billion gigabytes, or the equivalent of 237 billion fully loaded Amazon Kindle wireless reading devices, 4.8 quadrillion online bank transactions, 3 quadrillion Twitter feeds, 162 trillion digital photos, 30 billion fully loaded Apple iPod Touches, or 19 billion fully loaded Blu-ray DVDs.[6]

If each of us has ready access to only a minuscule fraction of this information, it is still unprecedented and difficult to comprehend. In fact, it is estimated that each and every day, a person is subjected to more new information than a person in the Middle Ages was in his or her entire lifetime.[7]

6. See EMC Corporation, "Digital Information Growth Outpaces Projections, Despite Down Economy," news release, May 18, 2009, http://www.emc.com/about/news/press/2009/20090518-01.htm. For a more complete picture and forecast, see John F. Gantz et al., "The Diverse and Exploding Digital Universe," IDC white paper, March 2008, http://www.emc.com/collateral/analyst-reports/diverse-exploding-digital-universe.pdf.

7. Alan C. Purves describes the move from print to digital forms of communication as the "third information transformation," citing the creation of writing in the seventh century bce and the invention

This level of information overload, mediated almost entirely by digital means, has fanned a relentless swirl of competing narratives and meaning-making systems that have, in turn, resulted in a number of interrelated and significant cultural shifts. Three of these shifts in particular deserve brief attention here in order to illustrate the changed context in which we preach and the challenges before us.

1. *We are moving from an age of obligation to an age of discretion.* A colleague of mine shared the following conversation he had with his daughter. She asked him why she should go to church when she "doesn't get anything out of it." He offered three reasons: first, God is worthy to be praised; second, other Christians receive something from your presence, even if you don't; and third, you do, in fact, get something out of it, even if you aren't aware of it: the sacramental gift of God's real presence in the Lord's Supper and the proclamation of the gospel.

Here is the—often generational—shift from being motivated by a sense of duty and obligation ("God is worthy to be praised"; "others need you there") to favoring our need, right, and ability to make choices with regard to what we call our discretionary time and income ("what's in it for me?" or, more generously, "what will I get out of this?"). While the impulse to question what we're getting out of something is often characterized as a generational narcissism, I think it has as much or more to do with the simple fact that there are so many more choices available that demand our attention. As Diana Butler Bass writes,

> Americans, even those of modest means, exercise more choices in a single day than some of our ancestors did in a month or perhaps even a year. From the moment we awaken, we are bombarded with choices—from caffeinated or decaffeinated, to flipping on any one of a hundred television stations as we ready the children for school, to getting our news in print, online, or via a mobile device, to what sort of spinach to buy to go with dinner (local, organic, fresh, frozen, chopped, whole leaf, bagged, or bunched).[8]

As a result, whereas in former times scarcity—in terms of products, opportunities, and information—was the limiting reality of much human interaction, today overabundance is the norm, and this has created a crisis of too many choices. As a consequence, time becomes the great limiting factor. In the

of the printing press in 1500 as the signature markers of the first two transformations. See *The Web of Text and the Web of God: An Essay on the Third Information Transformation* (New York: Guilford, 1998).

8. Diana Butler Bass, *Christianity after Religion* (San Francisco: HarperOne, 2013), 41.

face of this new reality, persons are increasingly less motivated by notions they have inherited about what they "should" do and more by a desire to get the most from the limited time amid the abundance of choices that confront them. Hence the family we referenced earlier suffers from over-commitment and assesses its participation in various groups in terms of what each group contributes to the family members' individual and familial life.

To offer another illustration of this shift, think for a moment of the generational difference in the motivation to make a pledge as part of a stewardship drive. While the sixty- or seventy-year-old will talk about our duty to the congregation and how the church needs our support, the thirty-something will more likely name the day-care center or various programs the congregation provides. Or think of how often senior members of your congregation, noting that when they were in their forties, they took on various leadership and servant roles in the church, ask you when the younger generation will "step up" and take on these same responsibilities.

These are examples of the shift from a generation motivated by duty to one motivated instead by discretion, and they indicate that the emerging generation of Christians will not come to church either because they feel they should or because their parents brought them. Rather, they will commit themselves only to those causes and communities that help them make sense of and navigate their lives in the complex, challenging, and fascinating world in which we live.

2. *We are moving from a time when identity was largely received to a time when identity is actively constructed.* The abundance of choices that has pushed us from a culture centered around duty to one focused on discretion has also affected how we construct our identity. Allow an extended illustration: When I grew up, there were three major television broadcast companies, and most of the programming was fairly similar: local and national news early in the evening, sitcoms that followed more or less the same format afterward, followed by dramas, etc. As a result, our viewing choices were relatively limited, and we therefore tended to watch whatever was on. Today, however, there are hundreds of television channels (I know, I know, and *still* nothing to watch!), not to mention on-demand movies and television via the Internet. Our choices for viewing have expanded exponentially, and it's no longer possible to just sit back and watch what's on, simply because we have to sort through so many options: major broadcasting networks as well as minor ones, networks that provide a variety of programming and those that are specialized (all sports, all news), networks that represent a broad range of views and those that intentionally represent a well-defined niche market.

Something very similar has happened with regard to the way we grow into our identity. For much of human history, "identity" wasn't a particularly meaningful category: you knew who you were by the family you were a part of and the way in which you earned a living, and these two were often closely related. After the Industrial Revolution and the rise of a middle class, identity became a topic of interest in diaries, letters, novels, and even sermons. Yet until very recently, the options available from which to construct one's identity were fairly limited, usually by factors of gender, education, ethnicity, and income. As a result, identity was something that was still fairly passively received. No longer. Today, the sources available from which we can construct our identity are manifold, and any kid with access to an iPod or the Internet has experienced this. For instance, when my mother went off to Gettysburg College sixty years ago, her two main vocational options (other than being a wife and mother, which were simply assumed) were to become a teacher or a nurse. In contrast, when my daughter goes to college six years from now, her vocational options will be nearly limitless.

So also when it comes to a variety of ways by which we define ourselves, not only in terms of work, but also in terms of interests, political affiliation, and religious—or, better, spiritual—expression. In fact, anytime you hear people saying they are "spiritual but not religious," this is in large part what they are saying: While they may share some of the interests in mystery or inclinations toward the divine that you have, they are not interested in simply receiving what feels to them like a prefabricated religious identity. Rather, they will figure things out for themselves, and there's a whole universe of digitally mediated resources to help them do just that.

3. We have moved from a culture that values tradition to one that values experience. The shift from receiving to constructing identity has in turn greatly affected our relationship to tradition. What is tradition, after all, if it is not our primary means by which to pass along our communal identity? But if we are now constructing our identity, tradition is far less important and certainly is not a source from which we gladly receive authoritative norms.

This isn't the only factor diminishing the importance of tradition. Over the last fifty years, we have experienced a slow erosion of trust in our major institutions caused by events like the Vietnam War, the scandals of Watergate and Enron, and disclosures of sexual abuse by clergy members and coaches. Because institutions—whether governmental, corporate, educational, or religious—are the key repositories and transmitters of tradition, when we lose trust in our institutions, we lose trust in the traditions they bear.

One further element of change that aligns with the thesis of this chapter is that we have now at our fingertips such a steady stream of instantaneous, 24/7 information that it seems not just outdated but actually foolish to put our trust in anything other than that ever-increasing and constantly updated pool of resources. Instantaneous news reports, the most recent product and film reviews, and the current status of just about anything are always just a keystroke or two away.

Given our immediate access to not just information but all kinds of digitally mediated experiences (personal interaction on social media, role-playing experiences via Second Life and other avatar-driven sites), it is perhaps not surprising that we increasingly privilege our present experience over any other source of authority in our lives.

The result is that while for centuries tradition preserved sets of social norms deemed critical to the identity and function of its groups, more recently tradition seems not only less necessary than it once did, but often downright contrary to the impulses of the digital age. "Tried and true" as a badge of trustworthiness is out, while "new and improved" and "on-demand" are in. Because of the degree to which tradition has been used to preserve the status quo, in fact, many in the digital age are suspicious of tradition, preferring their own experience as the arbiter of the good, the beautiful, and the true.[9]

Not that we don't like the *idea* of tradition. Everything from the popularity of *Antiques Roadshow* to the fascination with the royal wedding of William and Kate exposes our nostalgia for things that feel rich in tradition. But while we may yearn for the sense of stability that tradition lends, when it comes to making most of our daily decisions, even those that are rife with ethical consequences, we are far more likely to consult our iPhone than the teaching of our denomination or even our pastor.

SEIZING THE OPPORTUNITIES OF THE AGE

Before moving to illumine and suggest ways to grasp the opportunities resting within the challenges these cultural shifts present, I want to ask you a few questions. Have you noticed these three shifts in your own life, congregation, and community? Does naming them in this way help to explain some of the generational differences you've noticed, to interpret some of the challenges

---

9. For a story that captures our preference for our own judgment about goodness, God, and virtue rather than that of an established religious tradition, see Robert Bellah's 1985 description of "Sheilaism," the private faith of one woman named Sheila, in *Habits of the Heart: Individualism and Commitment in American Life* (Berkeley: University of California Press, 1996 [1985]), 220–21.

you've faced in recruiting participation in various aspects of your congregation's ministry, or to make sense of some of the conversations you've had with members as their commitment and attendance has slipped?

I ask because when I have presented this analysis to various groups of clergy, I have been struck by how it has resonated with their experience and provided useful labels for what many congregational leaders have been experiencing for some time. It's as if the phenomenon we have been experiencing isn't all that new, but rather that we're only just now recognizing how pervasive it is and finding ways to name and discuss it.

That invites another question: If these changes are as significant and omnipresent as I am suggesting, why have we been so slow to recognize them? I would suggest three reasons. The first is perhaps the least surprising. As church leaders, we ourselves tend to be motivated by a sense of duty and obligation, have inherited a relatively well-defined identity that has been useful to us in our work, and are part of a profession that loves and values tradition. The very things that prepare us to succeed in our vocations—at least as they have been defined for the last several centuries—are aspects of a culture that is quickly slipping away, so we have perhaps been susceptible to missing these changes.

Second, much of what we learned continues to work . . . pretty well . . . at least for a number of people. Generational and cultural change doesn't happen overnight, and many of the people we serve share our worldview and values. It may be that fewer and fewer of us exist, and that among the next generation the numbers will be sharply less, but at this point at least our rate of decline has been slow enough to make it easier to ignore the crisis we are most certainly in.

Third, as with the vast majority of adults, we are most comfortable with what we know, and we feel our anxiety rise sharply as we venture into areas where we feel less competent. To put it most bluntly, we continue to do things the way we were taught because that is what we know and trust and because we are surrounded by just enough people who feel the same way.

But for how long? While we may continue to find comfort and sustenance in the traditional ways of "doing church," most of us wonder whether our children and grandchildren will and, truth be told, fear that they will not. For this reason, and precisely because we love our church and congregations, many of us have been pushed to seek beyond the familiar in order to ask and try to answer a single, imperative question: How can we adapt our means of communication and community building so that God's life-giving gospel finds a hearing in this day and age?

That question brings me to the crux of this chapter: there rest within the very real challenges of this age significant opportunities to proclaim the gospel and kindle a more vibrant expression of Christian faith. While in the next chapter I will delve into the particular question of how our preaching might help us lay hold of these opportunities, I want to close this overview of our pluralistic world with four broad suggestions. After each suggestion, I will also frame an attending question to prompt deeper reflection on ways of thinking, being, and acting in this brave new world in which we find ourselves. While I hope the suggestions are helpful, I think wrestling with the questions in light of your own context may be even more important and, if we are willing to share what we are discovering, prompt a renewed conversation about how to be the church in this day and age.

1. *Focus on opportunities.* This is, in some ways, the theme of this chapter and book, but I want to emphasize the importance of focusing on opportunities not only in general but also with regard to the particular cultural shifts I've described. For example, while a sense of duty and obligation can be both important and useful, its emotional flip side is guilt. The flip side of discretion, however, is need. People are seeking to spend their time and energy in groups that meet their deep personal and spiritual needs.

Is meeting needs the be-all and end-all of human life? Of course not, but it's not a bad place to start if we want to invite people into a community that fosters transformation of life. Similarly, those identities we actively construct are typically those in which we are most invested. If we offer people the resources by which to help them create a meaningful religious identity in and through their relationship to Christ and Christ's church, they will own those identities far more than ones they simply inherited from their parents. As a result, they are likely to play a far more active role in sustaining the faith community that helped them construct a meaningful identity. Finally, while tradition tends to point us toward the past, experience invites us to glance to the present and future and can be a powerful motivating force.

Therefore, we might ask, what would our ministry and preaching look like if we imagined that the people coming are looking for a community that will help them meet their deepest needs, construct meaningful identities, and experience the living God?

2. *Start with questions.* We have a great message, one that has been passed down through the millennia. But it's time to admit that we don't have all the answers about how to either communicate it effectively or build an authentic community around that message. For this reason, we could learn a lot, and perhaps be taken more seriously, if we asked those currently attending our congregations—*and* those who do not attend—what they need from this community of faith. Take care, when you do so, not to frame the conversation

in terms of what the church isn't doing but rather what it might do, what it is doing well that could be strengthened, and what we dream of it being able to do. Cultivating this kind of positive and candid conversation can in itself greatly shape a congregation's spirit, level of self-awareness, and mission.

After this round of questions, invite another, this time of the surrounding community. Ask neighbors, shopkeepers, schoolteachers, retirees, youth, and business leaders what they need from a church. Don't be discouraged if they aren't all that familiar with your congregation. Instead, ask them what the community needs and how you could partner with them to make this community you share stronger.[10] Listen well, and allow this kind of conversation to guide you in dreaming about what God's preferred future for your congregation might be.

Ultimately, through that investigation we are asking this question: What would our congregation look like if we intentionally asked the people who are coming—and those who aren't—what we as a community need from our church?

3. Teach the biblical story. Let's face it. Our people barely know the biblical story, at least in a way that enables them to imagine it as a story in which they can find themselves. They may know parts of the Bible; that is, they may have a vague idea of the outline of Jesus' life, and they may be familiar with some of its stories, but what they know does not have the narrative integrity that would allow them to trace any semblance of a plot line from the beginning of the Biblical story at creation to its consummation at the end of time, let alone find themselves somewhere along the way as one of the active players in God's ongoing drama to love, bless, and save the world.

As we've already discussed, this isn't simply about biblical literacy but also and even more about biblical imagination: being able to see and recognize these stories as they are played out all around us at work and in play, at home and in schools, among our friends, family, and people around the globe. All of this means that the primary issue in the many ways we read and preach the Bible isn't figuring out the correct *meaning* of the passage we're reading but instead is *finding ourselves* in the passage. As we've seen earlier in this chapter, if we do not find the biblical drama to be a compelling story, we will not be able to invite people into genuine Christian identity. The imperative of offering this story as a meaningful, coherent, helpful resource requires us to rethink almost everything

---

10. In a sense, this is taking the conversation we had in the previous chapter a step further, as we move from focusing on and discerning individual vocation to considering the level of communal vocation.

about our ministry: our preaching, the use of the lectionary, our teaching, the way we invite people to read Scripture at home, and more.

Throughout our endeavor to nurture a more robust biblical imagination, this remains the question we are asking: What would church look like if it were the place where people hear God's story told, sung, and taught such that they can imagine themselves taking their place in that story?

4. *Tell a better story.* There are some enduring human needs that persist across cultures and generations and remain as important as ever during this digital age. We all need to belong; we all need to feel that what we do matters; we all need a clear sense of identity and crave that the world we live in makes sense; and so on. Knowing this, marketers across the world seek to tell us a story about how their product will meet those needs. The cars we drive, the clothes we wear, the food we eat, the shoes we lace, the computers we turn on—all of these now come with a story, and within that story a promise not simply about what the product can do, but about how the product can offer us meaning, joy, fulfillment, and a sense of dignity and worth. Many of these products are excellent and can be incredibly helpful. None of them, however, can deliver on the promises of meaning, community, identity, and self-worth.

The gospel message we have been commissioned to bear, however—the story of God's profound love for us and all the world—can and does offer these things. The problem isn't with the stuff, it's with what we've been led to believe we can expect from the stuff. We have a tremendous opportunity before us, therefore, to share the gospel, to give it away, to point to God's love, to make big promises, to dare great things so that people might be encountered by God and God's love and thereby find life. This is hard work, I know, but also good work, work worth giving our lives to.

Asking this question along the way may help: What would our church look like if it were the place where people are told they have infinite worth and are invited to join a community of persons devoted to discovering and sharing lives of meaning and purpose?

WRITING A DIFFERENT ENDING

Stories like the one I told at the beginning of this chapter about the family leaving church abound, as do the manifold predictions about the church's demise. But such predictions rarely come true, and not all the stories we hear have to end the same way. In fact, the one I started the chapter with had an unexpected conclusion.

After listening to his traveling companion for some time, my friend asked him whether he had told his pastor what he'd just shared. When the man admitted he hadn't, my friend urged him to, and he promised he would. About four months later, my friend received two e-mails. The first was from the pastor of his traveling companion, and it simply thanked my friend for encouraging the man to talk to him.

The second was from the man himself. He said that after he shared with his pastor his family's reasons for no longer going to church, his pastor asked if they could repeat that conversation on Sunday, during worship, in place of the sermon. After they did that, the pastor (in what I think was a tremendous act of courage) asked how many others felt the same way. In a worship service of just over a hundred people, more than a dozen hands went immediately into the air. So the pastor committed himself then and there to leading this congregation into a quest of how the biblical story might become useful to them, how it might inform their daily lives and decisions, and how the faith they professed on Sunday might help them sense God's presence and activity in their lives and community the rest of the week.

The e-mail closed simply, but profoundly: "So that's what we're doing. And you know what? We're in. We're staying."

The truth of the matter is that we don't finally know quite how to deal with the pluralistic world in which we now find ourselves. But we do have the capacity to listen, to learn, and to figure out again what it means to lead and live in this world as faithful Christians. Our role, in the end, is not that of pioneer or perfecter of the faith; another plays that role. We, rather, are called to be disciples, followers along the way. And if we open our eyes, ears, and hearts to give particular attention to where this path has led us just now—as delighted as we are surprised by the challenges and opportunities it presents us—we will, I believe, be well equipped not just to witness but also to participate in crafting an ending to our story that few currently expect. But then again, surprise endings are at the very heart of the story we tell.

6

Preaching and Christian Identity

Postmodernism, secularism, pluralism—these are significant and complicated topics, and I am grateful if you've been willing to wrestle with them. But while their antecedents, causes, and outcomes can at times feel as convoluted as they are complex, their influence in the lives of our people are often far more straightforward.

In recent years, for instance, I've been doing a lot of speaking about the phenomenon of "digital pluralism," which I described in the previous chapter. Much of this has been with pastors at various continuing-education events or theological conferences, and by and large, these pastors have appreciated a framework by which to name things they have been experiencing. I've also presented much of the same material in adult classes in congregations. There, too, I find lots of heads nodding as the folks in attendance find names and categories by which to make sense of their experience. But there is also a persistent question that gets asked, often after the presentation as people are leaving. It is a question that is as simple as it is poignant: Why don't my children and grandchildren go to church?

Of course, it's not just a question, it's also a lament, and I can almost always detect a note of grief in the voice of the questioner. During one adult forum I led, I was grateful not only that the gentleman who asked this question raised it during the class rather than afterward—so we could talk about it—but also that he continued and named what I think is often an unspoken second question. "When I was a kid," he began, "my parents took me and my brothers and sister to church, Sunday school, and confirmation. We all went to church our whole lives. When we had kids, we did the same: church, Sunday school, confirmation, and youth group. But many of our kids don't go to church anymore, and almost none of our grandkids do. So what happened?" And then came the question behind the question: "What did we do wrong?"

It's the same question we as pastors and preachers and church leaders often ask ourselves. What did we do wrong? But the fact of the matter is that we didn't do something wrong. The world just changed, and we haven't really changed with it. The world offered us so many other places to look for meaning and significance and identity, often in intriguing, challenging, and compelling ways. But we continued to offer Sunday school and confirmation as if there were no other options. We continued to do worship as if folks have nowhere else to go. And we continued to preach as if our people already know the biblical story and just need a little more instruction and inspiration to live it. But as we're discovering, that's hardly the case. We now have a generation of parents and their children who do not know the biblical story well enough to find it useful and who will not devote one hour a week to an activity unless it shapes and informs and gives meaning to the other 167 hours of their week.

Nor is it simply the younger generation that is drifting from church. Consider the following e-mail I received from a reader of my blog, ". . . In the Meantime," in response to some posts about how church as we know it does or does not serve us in nurturing our faith:

> I've been a Christian all my life. Our children are adults now; one almost finished with college and two already graduated with jobs in cities far away. My husband and I have found ourselves skipping church frequently, although we rarely missed while our children were home. I'm starting to realize that our church attendance was "for" our kids . . . they attended confirmation and youth group and church camp and leadership school, and we took them to church every Sunday. And I've found myself drifting and doubting . . . and church just doesn't seem relevant to my life. We frequently choose kayaking or biking over church attendance, feeling a little guilty as we do so.

I'll be honest, stories like this one make me as nervous about our future as do the mounting statistics about church decline or the rise of the "Nones," those folks who identify with no religious tradition whatsoever. Except that I'm not really just anxious about the church, I'm also anxious about my role as a leader in the church and, in particular, as one called to preach the gospel to this generation. As I said at the outset of this book, I've been preaching for more than twenty years and teaching preaching for over a decade. Yet in recent years, I've grown increasingly convinced that I don't really know how to preach anymore—at least not in a way that engages the children of my adult forum participant or the reader of my blog.

In saying that, I don't mean that what I was taught was *wrong*. It's more that the population for whom this kind of preaching works best is shrinking, while the population that doesn't seem drawn in by the practices I was taught seems only to grow. Indeed, at times it feels as though the world I was trained to preach to no longer exists. But as daunting as it is to admit this, it is also rather freeing. While a diagnosis is certainly not the same as a prescription, it is nevertheless an indispensable first step toward prescription, treatment, and renewed health.

For this reason, I have tried throughout this book to explain and explore some of these cultural shifts in order to provide a diagnosis of our condition. Moreover, at various points, I've made more prescriptive suggestions—some general, others more specific—that I hope are both encouraging and practical. At this point, though, I want to venture something more ambitious by beginning to chart the kind of new homiletic I believe responds to the postmodern, secular, and above all else pluralistic age we live in. While I wouldn't yet describe it as a comprehensive treatment plan, I am nevertheless excited about these preliminary steps. Moreover, I'm hopeful that if I share my thoughts with you, we might together engender a conversation about the changed and changing world in which we live and begin experimenting with our preaching for the sake of the proclamation of the gospel.

Preaching Upstream

Here's what you know: Mainline traditions have been in decline for the better part of the last half-century and have accordingly lost significant influence in North American culture.[1] During this same period, conservative and evangelical Protestant traditions have grown.

Here's what you may not know: Recent research suggests these two trends are *not* causally linked. It is not, in other words, that when mainline Protestants leave their congregations, they go to join conservative ones. Rather, when most mainline Protestants leave their congregations, they simply stop going to church altogether.[2]

---

1. As early as 1967, Peter Berger pointed to the "crisis of credibility" and "problem of plausibility" that traditional religious faith was experiencing. *The Sacred Canopy: Elements of a Sociological Theory of Religion* (New York: Anchor, 1967), 127ff.

2. The overwhelming cause of the disparate rates of growth is that birthrates among Evangelicals have been significantly higher than among mainline Protestants, although it appears that as the economic gap between Evangelicals and mainline Protestants closes, so does the gap in fertility rates. See Mark Chaves, *Congregations in America* (Cambridge, MA: Harvard University Press, 2004), 33–34.

But why do they stop going to church in the first place? Increasingly, researchers suggest that in a world saturated by meaning-making stories, the mainline church has failed to offer a compelling and central narrative identity that not only informs but also guides the lives of their congregants by providing a resilient religious identity. Thus, in a culture that values the individual's right to pursue religious fulfillment alongside life, liberty, and happiness, increasing numbers of mainline members discover numerous sources for their spiritual sustenance outside the walls of their congregations. Family, civic institutions, voluntary associations, and the embedded values and patterns of meaning inherent in them now exist side by side with local congregations as potential sources for spiritual identity.

This proliferation of valid spiritual resources represents a tremendous shift in the religious landscape. For the better part of the last three centuries, legitimate sources of religious identity have been few, with the local congregation preeminent among them. For this reason, and as we touched on in the preceding chapter, one's religious identity was far more a matter of passive reception than active construction. In the wake of the proliferation of spiritual options, that is no longer the case. And as we also discussed, the overabundance of options in our postmodern, 24/7 digital world—in terms of news, political ideas, and religious perspectives—compels persons, first, to recognize that there are multiple versions of reality coexisting and, second, to choose from among them. For this reason, as one scholar writes, "individuals must play a larger part in constructing their personal belief system" than ever before.[3]

Conservative churches have flourished amid this same proliferation of sources for religious identity by creating and maintaining a distinct "Christian worldview" that functions both as an internal norm for personal and corporate behavior as well as an external filter by which to assess competing religious claims. In the face of religious pluralism, conservative congregations have adopted a "traditionalist" stance that promotes a single, stable, and preferably unitary narrative identity that shields adherents from the tumult of competing truth claims.[4] Mainline congregations, in contrast, have consistently adopted a more "cosmopolitan" stance that values greater interpretive freedom and thereby leads to more variation—and consequently less cohesion—in narrative

---

3. Wade Clark Roof, *Community and Commitment* (New York: Elsevier North-Holland, 1978), 33.

4. While no tradition is entirely unitary (each will have proponents with differing interpretations), such variation in interpretation is discouraged. See Anthony Giddens and Christopher Pierson, *Conversations with Anthony Giddens: Making Sense of Modernity* (Stanford: Stanford University Press: 1998), 127–31.

identity.[5] Lacking the "strict code" of beliefs and behaviors prescribed by their more conservative counterparts, mainline congregations have had to compete in the marketplace of spiritual meaning and have often come up wanting.[6]

Interestingly, however—and perhaps contrary to popular belief, given numerous mainline arguments over social policies—the biblical and theological narrative mainline churches proffer has neither changed dramatically during these decades nor caused significant numbers of members to leave church.[7] Rather, mainline congregants simply no longer know that narrative well nor hold it as primary. Bereft of this primary narrative to supply a religious identity (or, rather, finding sources for a compelling identity from numerous narratives outside their congregations), many mainline members have lost any incentive to continue attending a church that doesn't meaningfully contribute to their understanding of, and life in, the world.

In this setting, one more easily appreciates the ambivalence of the preacher. Increasingly, if often unconsciously, we find ourselves offering interpretations of a narrative that few in the congregation know well enough to be able even to appreciate our interpretations, let alone to apply them to life outside the congregation's walls. Such an effort can feel like swimming upstream: it is cold and exhausting, and it yields little progress.

A generation ago, the dominance of the mainline Protestant worldview ensured numerous cultural reinforcements of the story preachers sought to interpret. Children learned it in school, artists from all genres drew upon it, national figures regularly invoked it, and even early television programs were permeated by it. Today, however, those supports have been all but stripped away. It's not that schools and popular culture no longer refer to Christian symbols and language, but rather that such language, placed alongside the linguistic systems of multiple religious and other meaning-making systems, is now ambivalent, ultimately testifying more to a pervasive religious relativism than to its original referent. Hence, and excepting the banal religious rhetoric

5. "Members [of liberal churches] often form beliefs with relatively little guidance from others and without benefit of rigidly prescribed doctrinal standards. Thus it is not surprising that they share so little in the way of consensus about the nature of Christian faith and the demands of commitment it places upon them." Roof, *Community and Commitment*, 33–34.

6. See Dean M. Kelley, *Why Conservative Churches Are Growing* (New York: Harper and Row, 1972/1977), 78–81.

7. See Chaves, *Congregations in America*, 34, and Ward Clark Roof and William McKinney, *American Mainline Religion: Its Changing Shape and Future* (New Brunswick, NJ: Rutgers University Press, 1987), 236–43.

of many politicians, unambiguous Christian conversation happens almost exclusively within the church.

Concurrent with the cultural decline of the Christian narrative, numerous other valid interpretive schemas have presented themselves. Many of them connect more directly to the lived experience of our congregants simply because they are promoted by the multiple channels our people regularly draw from: pop culture, news, the Internet, and more. Hence, while the mainline Christian story may appear alive and well within the walls of the congregation, outside the church all these other valid sources from which to construct a religious identity are giving traditional Christian faith a run for its money.

As a consequence, many of our people experience an enormous gap between their meaning-making experience on Sunday, when the dominant narrative is the biblical story, and on Monday through Saturday, when in the absence of an unambiguous Christian narrative they navigate through multiple other, and often more familiar, narratives. It is not that the Sunday sermon makes *no* sense, only that the sermon makes the *most* sense inside the church's walls, where it can be most easily connected with the larger story to which it refers.[8] The sermon, while meaningful, is greatly constrained in its applicability because the scope of the biblical narrative to which the sermon refers has itself been restricted to our life and identity in, rather than beyond, the church.

WEB 2.0 AND THE INTERACTIVE SERMON

I have identified the problem facing Christians in the twenty-first century as an overwhelming plethora of sources from which to construct religious identity, none of which hold a privileged place. This captures in a nutshell the reality of living in a postmodern, secular, and pluralistic world. Christian congregations will therefore thrive in this environment only to the degree that they offer the biblical narrative to their members as a creative and compelling resource with which to create an identity that brings greater understanding of both self and world and invites them to see God in their everyday lives. For this to happen, Christians churches cannot be content, as I've suggested, simply to promote biblical literacy (knowing the content of the Bible), but also and

8. As Thomas Long describes, "On the one side is the religious side of us, and on the other is the 'just trying to be human and make it through life' side. We go to worship, and we sing the hymns, pray the prayers, listen to the sermons, and then we go back out into the real world, where we have to deal with the mundane realities of life and make compromises and hard choices." *Testimony: Talking Ourselves into Being Christian* (San Francisco: Jossey-Bass, 2004), 39.

more importantly biblical *fluency* (the ability to think—without thinking—in the target language).

How might Christians develop this kind of fluency? Two options animate the contemporary religious scene. A conservative, traditionalist approach confronts the postmodern, pluralistic challenge by constructing a religious identity for its adherents that stands over and against other sources. Preaching, from this framework, is equal measures (1) teaching of the basic worldview and how to apply it to life and (2) exhortation to do so. The dominant homiletical preference of this orientation has naturally been expository preaching, where the preacher isolates the central cognitive idea of a passage so as to apply it to the life situation of the hearer today.[9] The enduring concern for traditionalist preachers is fidelity: has the sermon accurately and convincingly presented the cognitive truth embedded in Scripture? While this method has served conservative congregations well in recent decades, it is questionable whether it will continue to be able to stem the tide of multiple channels of meaning-making systems and possibilities that surround their members.[10]

In contrast, the mainline, cosmopolitan impulse has been to engage culture, confessing that the work of the triune God is manifest in culture as well as the church. Consequently, mainline preaching has been far more interested in facilitating an experience of God through its interpretation of the biblical text—preaching as event—rather than isolating a cognitive truth. Narrative preaching has lent itself to this goal by placing the biblical story alongside contemporary stories from art, culture, and current events so as to invite hearers to make experiential connections between the two.[11] The pressing concern for narrative preachers is not so much a rigid fidelity but instead relevancy: does the sermon help hearers make sense of the biblical story in light of their immediate context? While this method flourished when there were cultural structures in place to reinforce the biblical narrative, in recent years not only has it floundered absent such structures, but its very affirmation of multiple contemporary stories as sources of religious identity has contributed to relativizing its own message.

---

9. See Haddon Robinson, *Biblical Preaching: The Development and Delivery of Expository Messages*, 2nd ed. (Grand Rapids: Baker, 1991).

10. "The rate at which evangelicals lose people to secularity and to religions other than Protestantism, though still lower than for moderate and liberal Protestants, is increasing." Chaves, *Congregations in America*, 34.

11. See Edmund Steimle, Morris Niedenthal, and Charles Rice, *Preaching the Story* (Philadelphia: Fortress Press, 1980).

It would seem that we have reached an impasse: either adopt a rigid formulation of a Christian narrative that negates much if not most of the cultural forms we live with, or affirm those cultural forms at the expense of the primacy and even relevancy of the biblical narrative as constituent to our religious identity. It's at just this point that turning to recent trends in the ongoing development of the Internet may be instructive.

In many ways, the Internet epitomizes the relativistic world of competing value systems and sources for religious identity in which we preach. The ability to click between alternating, even opposing narratives instantaneously captures the essence of lives in a digitally pluralistic world. While we may visit the website of our local congregation or national denomination, we know those sites are only two of literally millions that offer the resources from which to construct a compelling narrative identity.

Over the last decade, however, observers of the Internet have noticed an increasing preference among users not only to receive information but also to interact with it. A dozen years ago, this was represented by the growing phenomenon of chat rooms; today you see it in social networks like Facebook, e-commerce sites like eBay and Amazon, which rely heavily upon user ratings of their experiences, the immense success of a volunteer-driven encyclopedia like Wikipedia, and the actual cooperative production of open-source software. Even now, this kind of interaction is being pushed further, as Second Life and similar avatar-driven, virtual worlds allow users to construct and experiment with multiple digital identities.

The heightened value that users assign to interacting with and through computer programs has not gone unnoticed by software developers. Recognizing that interactive use not only leads to greater fluency with and allegiance to particular Web-based platforms like Twitter, but also leads to better technology as in open-source programs like Mozilla Firefox, programmers have increasingly designed software that is not "complete" apart from user interaction, adaptation, and improvisation. This emerging trend has been named Web 2.0, a term first coined by Darcy DiNucci. Writing in 1999, DiNucci predicted, "The Web we know now, which loads into a window on our computer screens in essentially static screenfuls, is an embryo of the Web as we will know it in not so many years . . . [when] the Web will be understood, not as screenfuls of text and graphics but as a transport mechanism, the ether through which interactivity happens."[12]

12. Darcy DiNucci, "Fragmented Future," *Print* 53, no. 4 (1999), 32. You can find the article on the Web at http://www.cdinucci.com/Darcy2/articles/Print/Printarticle7.html.

I am intrigued by the possibility Web 2.0 holds as a metaphor for an approach to bridging the gap between the identity and meaning making that we experience on Sunday and that of the rest of the week. For instance, what if we imagined that the purpose of Sunday worship, and in particular the sermon, was not to present "screenfuls of text"—a finished message, an artful interpretation of the biblical text—but instead as "a transport mechanism, the ether through which interactivity happens." What if the sermon provided not simply the content of the biblical narrative as a source for religious identity, either in the "strict" prescriptive form of conservative preaching or in the "lenient" suggestive form of mainline preaching, but also promoted lively interaction with that story? To put it another way, is there room in our homiletical imagination for an interactive sermon?

Most, if not all, mainline preachers earnestly wish and sometimes exhort our hearers not only to apply their faith to their lives but also to share that faith with others. But how can we expect our hearers to accept our invitation unless we also provide them the means and occasion by which to practice what we invite? It is precisely the gap between our experience of Sunday and the rest of the week that makes it nearly impossible for most mainline churchgoers to imagine applying or sharing their faith. Even if they know the biblical narrative (literacy), they have little competency or confidence in connecting it meaningfully to the tasks of everyday life (fluency). Moreover, if our people have spent their entire lives watching others (the preacher) talk about faith but have never themselves had an opportunity to do so, where will they have developed the competence and confidence to do it themselves?

Participatory Preaching

Because the sermon is the most unscripted part of the worship service, it presents itself as an ideal candidate to provide the arena in which hearers can not only hear the biblical story but also grow in their ability to make sense of their lives in light of it. The goal is that, over time, hearers discover in Scripture a valid, compelling, and useful meaning-making narrative that helps them make sense of all the other options and stories in our postmodern, pluralistic world.

To help them grow toward such competence, I believe we will need to shift from what I would describe as a performative homiletic to a participatory one.[13] In a performative homiletic, the preacher is the chief and often sole

---

13. In recent years, there have been several salutary treatments of the relationship between preaching and performance. See, for instance, Jana Childers and Clayton Schmit, eds., *Performance in Preaching: Bringing the Sermon to Life* (Grand Rapids: Baker, 2008) and similar monographs by contributors to this

interpreter of Scripture. The emphasis is almost entirely upon the preacher's role to study, interpret, and proclaim the text in our hearing. At its best, performative preaching "renders" the biblical text, making a passage written thousands of years ago three-dimensional, contemporary, and compelling.

As desirable as this most certainly is, however, it does not necessarily equip hearers to do this kind of interpreting for themselves in everyday life. Further, it may have the unintended consequence of impeding the hearers' facility at interpretation either by promoting the preacher as the professional interpreter (in which case the hearer has no need to interpret) or by setting the bar for competent interpretation dauntingly high (in which case the hearer does not dare interpret for fear of failure).

On this next point I want to be most clear: it's not that a performative homiletic is wrong; artful interpretation of the text is only to be esteemed. Rather, the performative homiletic is simply *insufficient* in and of itself to the demands of the day and therefore must be supplemented by a homiletic that invites, nurtures, and expects a lively interaction between hearer and text. Here we are perhaps not far from Kierkegaard's oft-quoted affirmation that while most of us assume that in the divine drama of worship the minister is the performer, God the prompter, and the congregation the audience, in genuinely biblical worship God is the audience, the congregation the performers, and the minister the prompter.[14] But if we don't provide our people the chance to practice lively and useful interpretation of the biblical story in the relatively safe space of the sanctuary, how can we expect them to do so in their daily lives amid all the competing contenders for religious identity?

And I don't think I'm alone. Several developments in homiletical and theological literature in recent years signal openness to this move and provide assistance in making it. I will mention four briefly:

> 1. In his *Preaching Jesus*, Charles Campbell invites us to "build up the church" by training hearers to understand and use the distinct language of the Christian faith so that through diligent practice our hearers can re-describe the world in terms of the patterns and figures of the biblical narrative.[15]

volume. While I recognize that none of these authors advocates a homiletic that privileges the preacher over the hearer in the act of interpretation, the metaphor of "performance," while certainly highlighting a valid dimension of preaching, nevertheless shifts attention to the preacher as the primary "performer" in the "divine drama" enacted in the sermon.

14. Søren Kierkegaard, *Purity of Heart Is to Will One Thing* (San Francisco: HarperOne, 1956), 180–81.

15. "A genuinely new hearing will require more than the technique of the preacher; it will also require a disciplined community of hearers grounded in the practice of Scripture, sacrament, and discipline."

2. John McClure and Lucy Rose have both advocated for including hearers in the interpretive work leading up to the preaching, with Rose inviting the participation of all of the gathered assembly in the proclamation.[16]
3. Several theologians have taken up the topic of "Christian practice" to good effect, and those works open the door to conversation regarding how preaching can foster authentic Christian practice.[17]
4. Thomas Long provides guidance to Christians seeking to speak and share their faith in the many venues that constitute their everyday lives.[18]

Given these encouraging developments, I think it's high time that we move equipping our hearers to be competent, even fluent interpreters of the Christian faith to the center of our conversations about preaching. Toward this end, I offer the following handful of suggestions that invite greater participation in the sermon and engagement with the biblical story.

1. *Visit people in the venues of their Christian vocations—at home, work, school, places of volunteer activity, and more.* While we discussed this in greater detail in a previous chapter, I want to say again that I think there is simply no better way to relate one's preaching to the real lives of our congregants and thereby model making connections between faith and life than by knowing more about congregants' "real lives" and referring to these in the sermon.

2. *Invite congregants to leave worship to "look for" the biblical message they just heard interpreted in their daily lives.* Where, that is, do we see a prodigal son (or daughter) in our midst, and what would it mean to run out to receive him or her back? In what ways are we tempted like Adam and Eve to secure for ourselves knowledge of the future to dispel our native insecurity apart from relationship with God? Even framing the outcome of the sermon in these terms—equipping

Campbell, *Preaching Jesus: New Directions for Homiletics in Hans Frei's Postliberal Theology* (Grand Rapids: Eerdmans, 1997), 247. The primary work of biblical interpretation in the church, however, rests with the preacher, who is the one to "perform" or "enact" Scripture and, in particular, the story of Jesus (see pp. 211–20).

16. See John S. McClure, *The Roundtable Pulpit: Where Leadership and Preaching Meet* (Nashville: Abingdon, 1995); and Lucy Atkinson Rose, *Sharing the Word: Preaching in the Roundtable Church* (Louisville: John Knox Press, 1997), esp. p. 123.

17. See, for instance, Dorothy C. Bass, *Practicing Our Faith. A Way of Life for a Searching People* (San Francisco: Jossey-Bass, 1997/2010); and Diana Butler Bass, *The Practicing Congregation: Imagining a New Old Church* (Herndon, VA: Alban Institute, 2004). See also Thomas G. Long and Leonora Tubbs Tisdale, eds., *Teaching Preaching as a Christian Practice: A New Approach to Homiletical Pedagogy* (Louisville: Westminster John Knox, 2008).

18. Long, *Testimony: Talking Ourselves into Being Christian* (San Francisco: Jossey-Bass, 2004).

people to make use of the biblical stories to interpret their lives—may stretch our own preaching.

3. *Invite congregants not only to look for the biblical stories they are listening to but also to e-mail you and tell you what they have seen.* Or perhaps you can hold an occasional Sunday adult class where you look ahead to coming texts and check back in regarding what people have been finding. However you do it, plan to incorporate some of what you have learned in a future sermon, and tell folks that you plan to do so to encourage them to look, see, and report. Commission your hearers, that is, to be your eyes and ears in the world, reporting to you some of what they see to broaden your own pastoral and homiletical perspective and view.

4. *Besides inviting people to participate after the sermon (looking for the biblical stories and characters in their lives) and before the sermon (sharing their thoughts and observations about upcoming texts with you), consider also inviting participation during the sermon.* This, quite frankly, is where most of us—preachers and listeners alike—get nervous. The first kind of participation I'd suggest is nonverbal. This might be by inviting simple exercises like printing out the passage and inviting people to underline the words or phrases that stick out to them. It might be an invitation to write down a question they have on a three-by-five card and place it in the offering plate. Or perhaps it's an invitation for them to write down a central element of the sermon—that they are God's people sent to care for the world—and inviting them to carry it with them. Or perhaps it's a matter of inviting people to raise their hands as they choose among various answers to a question you pose. The idea at this point is simply to give congregants a low-level way to participate in the sermon that should not be terribly anxiety-provoking.

5. *As the congregants (and preacher) develop confidence in participating in the sermon, occasionally take time during the sermon to have listeners share with each other where they see connections between the biblical passage and their lives.* It may be helpful, particularly for introverts, to prepare some tablets of paper so that those who are not ready to participate in conversation might journal their reflections. But the goal over time is to help folks grow comfortable with interpreting the Bible and sharing their reflections verbally.

6. *During different parts of the worship service, invite persons to share some of the connections they are making between their faith and their daily lives.* They can certainly offer the "mission moment" or "temple talk" or any of the various other ways we encourage laypeople to speak during church. But I would also encourage us to invite our people to talk about their faith during the sermon.

One congregation I know regularly gives over the season of Epiphany, for instance, to sermons that are shaped around a prepared interview between the pastor and a congregant regarding the appointed text and how it affects the congregant's life in the world.

7. *From time to time, have this kind of sharing not only occur during the sermon but be offered as the sermon.* Invite, that is, one or more persons to make connections between the biblical passage appointed for the day and their daily lives. Meet with them ahead of time, study the passage together, and provide resources, but then allow their interpretations not only to illustrate the sermon but actually to *be* the sermon. Few things will be more effective in boosting people's confidence than a chance to share their faith in public. Moreover, the power of such an example for the rest of the congregation is hard to underestimate. In seeing someone "just like them," as opposed to the "trained professional," speak about his or her faith, our people begin to cultivate an imagination that they can do this, too. And with practice, they can.

As you've no doubt noticed, these options for participation increase in terms of what they expect from participants. And while these seven suggestions aren't offered as a prescription, I think there's some merit in considering initially starting with exercises that require less direct participation from our people. As they (and you) get used to this way of engaging the biblical text and as they (and you) gain confidence that they really can do this, you can move to higher levels of participation. Small steps sometimes move us forward more quickly than giant bounds.

But while a measured introduction to participatory preaching could be spread over several months or even a year, your people might adjust to a more active role in the sermon faster than we may think. After all, many of them have probably tweeted about presidential election debates, "liked" any number of products on Facebook in the last month, or checked in on a friend's cancer treatment via CaringBridge. Given their familiarity with the interactive character of life in a Web 2.0 world, they may take these shifts in worship in stride and even appreciate your efforts to engage them more actively.

There are, of course, other places in the worship service (the prayers of the people, for instance) and congregational life (adult and youth education) where we can invite people to gain experience in bridging the gap between the biblical narrative and their daily lives. But the prominence and public nature of the sermon make it an ideal place to move from passive to active identity construction. If we can imagine making a leap similar to that made by users and programmers who left the static world of Web 1.0 to inhabit the more dynamic and interactive world of Web 2.0, we might be able to offer the sermon as, indeed, a "transport mechanism, the ether through which interactivity [between God's word and God's people] happens."

If so, our people might soon find themselves not just listening to the sermon, but actually creating it along with you. And that role as participant and co-creator may just lead to a more robust, intentional, and valued Christian identity even—or, perhaps, especially—in a pluralistic world.

Afterword: The Long and Winding Road

After climbing down that embankment away from the bull and getting back into the cold white water, I ended up body-rafting for another mile or two down through the ravine until the river eventually widened and slowed, so I could swim to a nearby bank and wait for my family to catch up in the raft. By that time, I was cold, drenched, pretty tired, and truth be told, a bit chastened.

But above and beyond all that, I was also exhilarated. It had been a challenge, no question, but I came out of that experience with some hard-won experience (hold the raft much tighter!) that made the rest of the trip incredibly fun. I also emerged with a keener sense of confidence in what my twelve-year-old self could do. I won't say I left at the end of the day in love with the Roaring Fork River, but I did respect it—and myself—more than I had previously.

That's my hope for our venture into the uncharted waters of a world that is simultaneously postmodern, secular, and pluralistic: that we might allow our experience in the culture to challenge us and at times chasten us, as well as renew our confidence both in ourselves as preachers and also—and even more so—in the gospel we have been called to preach.

There are times, of course, when I wish things had not changed or that I at least knew just what to do. But there are other times when I feel the same rush of exhilaration as I did on that warm and sunny summer afternoon thirty-five-odd years ago. Because whatever world we grew up in, whatever world we were trained for, this is the world we are living in now. More than that, this is the world that God loved so much as to send God's only Son, Jesus, to announce God's commitment to love, bless, and save just this world.

So while I haven't given you answers, let alone quick fixes, to the questions and challenges that beset us, I do hope you sense an invitation: an invitation to lean into the mystery of this age so we might embrace it together, walking forward with confidence that if we are attentive both to the spirit of the age and the Spirit of Christ, a more fitting homiletical response will suggest itself in time.

In the meantime, however, there is still much to do. Waiting upon the Spirit is not idle time. Rather, I hope you will be encouraged by my analysis, hunches, and suggestions to try out some homiletical experiments of your own to see what might prompt a fresh hearing of the gospel in this day and age. But here we should be both clear and honest: with experiments come failures. So I hope you also sense an invitation not just to experiment, but also to fail.

To be perfectly candid, I wasn't trained to fail. Indeed, there are times I think that most of my education was geared toward avoiding failure. But I've been convinced that failure, as least *smart* failure, should be our constant companion and ready ally in this changed and changing world. As eminent physicist Niels Bohr once said, an expert is nothing more than a professional who has failed in every possible way in a given discipline. Little wonder, then, that many of the most progressive and entrepreneurial companies today hold as a primary motto, "Fail faster!" The quicker we are to experiment and fail, the quicker we are to learn our context well enough to succeed. So it's my hope and expectation that if we can fashion a community of "homiletical entrepreneurs," we will together discover the means by which to give adequate expression to the gospel of God in this day and age.

Lest we are tempted at times to lose heart on this journey, it may be helpful to remember that we are only the latest in a long line of preachers who struggled to understand the context sufficiently to sound forth the peculiar but compelling promises of God. From Paul standing at Mars Hill glancing upon idols to every god imaginable to him, to the suburban preacher who looks out at graying heads and wonders where all the people went, it is both our duty and delight to survey the scene, make our wager about what constitutes fit and faithful testimony, and then risk ourselves and our faith in the attempt to preach the Word.

Whether we succeed or fail, however, it is the Word that both commissions us and seals our hope. For whatever path we venture at this particular crossroads, still our hope is secured not by our success but by the one who hung on the cross for our sins and was raised again for our justification. So let us venture forth in confidence and expectation, boldness and humility, down this long and winding road.

If you are willing to join me, know that I am grateful for your company. And perhaps as we set out, we would be well served by taking on our lips the classic prayer from Matins: "Lord God, you have called your servants to ventures of which we cannot see the ending, by paths as yet untrodden, through perils unknown. Give us faith to go out with good courage, not knowing where we go, but only that your hand is leading us and your love supporting us, through Jesus Christ our Lord. Amen."